Hidden Disabilities

(Revised 2022 Edition)

*Challenging institutional unfairness
and encouraging the faith.*

PAUL TREACY

WESTBOW
P R E S S®
A DIVISION OF THOMAS NELSON
& ZONDERVAN

WestBow Press books may be ordered through booksellers or by contacting:

WestBow Press
A Division of Thomas Nelson & Zondervan
1663 Liberty Drive
Bloomington, IN 47403
www.westbowpress.com
844-714-3454

Scripture taken from the King James Version of the Bible.

ISBN: 978-1-6642-3547-2 (sc)
ISBN: 978-1-6642-3546-5 (e)

Print information available on the last page.

WestBow Press rev. date: 09/09/2022

Contents

PART THREE

Acknowledgements

Thank you to the following who have been incredibly supportive of me:

My family - From both near and far. Keith & Margaret Oliver, Kevin Ludkin, Jonathan & Heather Brain, James Gardiner, 'Pepsi' Cara Simmens, Martyn Brown, Keith & Sharon Wilson, Liam Berry, Vaz & Debbie Smith, Wayne & Marie-Innocence Lawther, Nigel Grima, Margaret Woolford, Dave & Bev Watkins, Rufus Araoye, Geoff & Jackie Gale, Mark Collier & the Staff of HEALS & Wiltshire Mind, past & present.

Preface

During the latter part of 2020 & early 2021, after months into the Coronavirus Pandemic, I had been flirting with the idea of trying to write my very own Christian book. I had been spending much more time alone than at any other time of my life & without even having so much as a cat or a dog for company. Would it even be possible for me, of all people, to even be able to write one? And if I did, would I actually be taken seriously enough?

Nine years previously, I wrote a book called 'Team HEALS', in reference to HEALS, a charity based in the nearby, historic town of Malmesbury, that I was a founding member of, and I started to write it on the very same day that the Olympic torch was taken through my hometown of Chippenham in May 2012. The flame passed through many towns & cities in the run up to the London 2012 Olympics. That historic day in my town was itself, the starting part to the book.

Sadly, it never got to print but I always held hope that I could always try writing another book, possibly some other day. While I obviously did not enjoy the loneliness, which at times was really tough, it certainly did give me plenty of more time to think.

Introduction

I was not diagnosed as being with Autism until I was 33 years old back in 2010. It came as no surprise as my then 6 year old son, Joseph, was diagnosed several years beforehand in his preschool years. There was much relief but also much anger that I hadn't been diagnosed in my own childhood years. I could have maybe gone on to do so much more had there maybe been more adequate support out there for me.

There are countless 'what ifs' regarding the many, many unfair setbacks that I have encountered over the years. But what's done is done. I know that this continuous way of thinking would consume me with bitterness. With the help of God and some really valuable people, I know that my relationship with the Lord & helping others is the right way to go.

However, no matter how hard I try, never a single day now goes by, thinking about what I could have done - Should have done - before reaching my 40th Birthday, had just 3-4 things been different and more in my favour, during my more earlier years.

Alas, there are no memories or pictures of me before my 40th Birthday, graduating at Cambridge, of my glorious Summer Wedding day with my Christian Wife & meeting cheery, Church Ministers during visits to Uganda and Kenya - As none of them ever happened. Though I still consider myself to be truly blessed, despite the psychological damage I have endured over my lifetime.

I have reasonably good, physical health, (though could do with shedding a few pounds) been fortunate to have visited some amazing places & have been fortunate enough to have met some fantastic, famous Christians such as 1980s pop singer, Yazz & Paul Jones of Manfred Mann fame.

Naturally, I am a strong advocate of issues like mental health awareness, child protection and promoting awareness and reforms of many kinds, as well as raising awareness of hidden disabilities. I truly despise all forms of persecution & injustices anywhere on Earth from systemic, Third World corruption to modern Slavery and to even the broken & costly, American, industrial prison complex. Around 65% of the 2.3 million US inmates would benefit more from receiving mental health support & drug rehabilitation, rather than being trapped in a continuous, cycle of incarceration.

While churches of all denominations have made great strides over the last 20 years with the advent of foodbanks, homelessness support, more stringent, child safeguarding procedures & 'Messy Church' schemes, more understanding on the issues of hidden disabilities and how best to accommodate such people would go a very long way indeed. Some churches do have resources available but I have made recommendations of my own from my own experiences.

For the record, I have decided it would be best not to mention Aspergers Syndrome & the phrase 'Aspie', its shorter variant. There has been much debate in recent years that Dr Hans Asperger, the Austrian paediatrician after whom the condition was named, may have been complicit in Nazi era crimes. Nor do I wish to discuss the Byzantine, UK benefits system and the Catch 22 situations that I have often found myself in.

I truly hope that you will enjoy this book. Please keep in mind that I have no titles to my name or Theology degree of any kind. This is a huge leap of faith for me. Whether it can make any shred of difference, who knows. I could well be 'bringing coals to Newcastle' in writing this. (An old English saying, implying that you have not made any kind of difference, have laboured in vain, etc.) However, if this book can encourage just one person to Jesus, prevent one suicide or change someone's perception on Autistic and vulnerable people, then it will all be completely worth it.

Paul Gerrard Solomon Treacy, March 2021.

PART ONE

England's Grim Underbelly

During the time the original copy of this book went to print for the first time, the 'Euro 2020' European soccer championships tournament, which was delayed by a full year due to the pandemic, was already underway. The tournament, which is usually hosted by one or two nations, was played throughout the entire European continent with even the city of Baku, many miles away in the former Soviet Republic of Azerbaijan being one of the host cities. Wembley Stadium, London hosted the most amount of games during the tournament including both Semi Finals and the Final.

The England national team exceeded everyone's expectations, despite not having the best of starts, beating old adversaries Germany along the way and managing to reach the Final. This was the first time England had reached any Cup Final in 55 years since they won the World Cup back in 1966.

England faced Italy in the Final and the national excitement reached Fever pitch levels not seen in many people's lifetimes. After an amazing start with England leading 1-0 very early on, Italy scored an equaliser midway through the second half and after a 1-1 draw at full time, the game went into extra time - And with the score still level, came the dreaded penalty shootout, which Italy won and they were Crowned the tournament Champions.

Each of the 3 players who missed our penalties were black players. Very sadly, each of them, Marcus Rashford, Jadon Sancho and Bukayo Saka, were then subjected to a torrent of horrendous, often racist abuse on social media. Many of those dishing out the vile abuse received 'likes' on their accounts. A mural of Marcus Rashford in his home city of Manchester in the Withington area he grew up in, was defaced with racist graffiti. Marcus Rashford himself has done much in recent times in urging the Government to do more to campaign for better social equality and to help Britain's most deprived families, having grown up himself in poverty and with his Mother, Melanie, holding down several jobs to make ends meet before he managed to break into the Manchester United first team as a teenager.

The overwhelming majority of fans and general public were very rightly outraged at the vitriol aimed towards these fantastic, young men. The Rashford mural, within hours of the vandalism, was adorned with messages of support coming from across the country, with the graffiti, first covered up then later removed by professional artists. Over the following weeks, the Police made numerous arrests. Many of those who wrote derogatory messages online were not always of the stereotype of shaven headed, tattooed yobs from sink estates. A good few of them were well educated and from very respectable backgrounds. The final was also marred by hundreds of ticketless 'fans' trying to break into the Stadium and with scenes of hooliganism stretching from the Wembley area to Central London. Some will argue that these thugs are only a minority but it is still too large a minority for comfort. The fact that some young adult men young enough to be my own son can send monkey emojis to black footballers and dismiss it as mere 'banter' is a huge cause for concern.

I personally believe that in all of the White majority nations on this Earth, the United Kingdom, Inc Northern Ireland is probably among the top 3-4 of the most tolerant and welcoming for ethnic minorities in this current day and age. Attitudes have slowly and gradually improved. Mixed race relationships for instance, are more socially acceptable among the general British population than they used to be, prior to 1995. White women in my parents generation were far more likely to be disowned by their families for being in relationships with black men and other minorities.

Tyrone Mings, who currents plays for Aston Villa at this current time, my Dad's team, played in some England first team games during the 'Euro 2020' tournament, hails from my hometown of Chippenham and is of mixed heritage himself. Believe it or not, I can remember him as a boy and he was often in the stands watching and cheering the local team. His Father, for several seasons played for and for a while was the Manager of Chippenham Town Football Club. (A great, family friendly Club which even has a small, Norwegian fan base.)

What exactly has all of this got to do with the subject of Hidden Disabilities anyway, you might ask? Among the people that Marcus Rashford is trying to help, a fair percentage among them will have hidden and/or physical disabilities. In order to tackle the racism among the small, moronic minority you also need to tackle every other type of Prejudice out there. Much of it stems from outdated attitudes that are sometimes passed down the generations and from certain sections of the downmarket, tabloid media which is drip fed to the readers of this garbage on a regular basis.

Marcus Rashford has often been berated for his campaigning off the pitch and seen as having a 'chip on his shoulder' and having 'a bit of an attitude' for pressurising the UK Government and highlighting issues about modern British poverty and for more adequate, long term help for those in need. Marcus has often been met with typical responses on social media that if certain families can't feed their children then they shouldn't breed them and that such families squander their money on cigarettes, alcohol and plenty of 'nice things' - a vulgar stereotype that is simply not true for the vast majority of people genuinely struggling to get by. Most of those people who have the 'nice things' such as a large TV screen and higher grade, brand name clothing would have probably purchased such items when times were better for them.

Which brings the subject of those deemed to be 'playing the system' - Eg: Welfare fraudsters. Many people often have suspicions of those who are on benefits and especially people with physical and hidden disabilities, often spurred on by certain sections of the media, which can lead to verbal and sometimes physical abuse towards disabled people. There is a 'deserving' poor and 'undeserving' poor mindset that has been around in this country since the Victorian era. Certain newspapers crop up stories, every so often, of workshy, troublesome couples with over eight children who are a nightmare for their neighbours and of fraudsters, being jailed and/or heavily fined after claiming to have had debilitating health problems for years but were being investigated by the authorities (after being tipped off) after seen regularly socialising in pubs, having lavish holidays and playing 18 rounds of golf. Such stories are the exception and most certainly not the norm. Examples, such as these are to be found at the very most extreme 1,000/1 end of the scale.

For people who don't have a faith, their view on the less fortunate people will usually depend on their own life's experiences, such as their own upbringing and their political leanings. In many instances, their points of view will be shaped by what media outlets and/or newspapers that they generally tend to get their regular information from. For me, I have been on both sides of the scale in a 'Gullivers Travels' kind of way, in what has been commonly termed by a fair percentage of the British press as the 'workers versus shirkers' debate. It must be duly noted that I have never been a 'shirker' – a vulgar and unpleasant form of rhetoric. And, with the exceptions of illnesses, I have always been productive in one capacity or another, by volunteering in my spare time, helping family members and others, which I try to do whenever I can.

On so many occasions, I can often recall, from the mid 1990s to the majority of the 2000s, driving home from work or returning home on the bus after a very rough shift: My limbs would be aching all over, the tee shirt I was wearing underneath would be stuck to my skin with sweat. I would sometimes be filling up with rage, on top of the job dissatisfaction, while driving by and often seeing the same people of working age in the same areas who were obviously not working themselves and who, to me at least, seemed to be carefree and enjoying their day. Here I am toiling away and paying my taxes for the likes of them to lounge about, I thought.

After my 2008 job redundancy, I can often remember struggling to get out of bed until 11am. This was not through laziness but because of struggling with crushing, mental health issues at the time. There would be little for me to look forward to during most days, during much of the late 2000s and early 2010s, especially through the Winter months. Having to go to the Job Centre to sign on and explain every fortnight what I was doing to try and look for work was always a horrible and humiliating experience for me. Time and time again, I would send off application forms and not even get the courtesy of a reply. Before I actually knew it, I would have guys in cars and unmarked vans honk their horns, shout and make gestures at me, as they would assume I wasn't working when I was out and about on weekday afternoons.

Though I never resorted to honking and gesturing at others myself, as it is cowardly and unpleasant behaviour, I now feel horrible pangs of guilt in how I viewed those people I often seen about, sat on benches, while I was driving/on the bus, going home from work in previous times. The majority of them looked vulnerable and were highly unlikely to ever be employed by any firm anyway. Maybe they too had disabilities both hidden and physical? There are numerous hidden, physical disabilities too such as Cystic fibrosis, Chron's disease and Spinal disorders. Those whom I thought had a 'cushy' life, such terminology and rhetoric is often typically used by the mainstream media, may very well have been in regular discomfort and reliant on heavy medication. They may possibly have suffered from life changing injuries or struggle with Post Traumatic Stress Disorder after serving in combat, possibly somewhere in the Middle East. Who knows? (No child nowhere, during their school years, ever say that they actually want to do absolutely nothing after leaving school and go 'on the dole' – Claim welfare - Even if their parents and older siblings are.)

I will not claim to have a huge amount of knowledge on sociology. We are all products of our environment, which will shape us in our thoughts and actions, throughout the course of our lives. However, it is common knowledge that once you get beyond a certain distance of usually 100 miles from London and South East England, life for the less fortunate becomes far more tougher and the chances of betterment for such people becomes far less likely. More investment typically goes into London and the surrounding, affluent, home counties like Surrey and Hertfordshire while communities elsewhere, like those north of Birmingham, most of which were once industrious, are often left to suffer.

Germany and Japan may have been the main defeated nations during World War Two but both have actually fared better than Britain in so many ways since the 1990s. Why is this? There are various reasons for this but much of it stems from the mindsets within them. There is less of a class structure in these respective nations than here and more fair play at hand. As far as I know, there are no foodbanks in either nation and absolutely no regions in either nation where poverty is on a par with Middlesbrough/Teeside, Glasgow or the former mining towns of South Wales.

Autistic people and more vulnerable folk are among certain sections of society that, more often than not, are blamed for much of what is going wrong within these borders: That we are a 'ball and chain' holding this nation back from possible, greater prosperity and achievement when the real truth is that it is actually WE who are held back and then we get the blame when we are denied the chance to show our true colours.

Let's REALLY put things into perspective here: We are not to blame for the way countless Billions of taxpayers money gets totally squandered, year on year at local and national level via bureaucracy, corruption and incompetence of all sorts. Not to mention so many vanity projects of all kinds. Just in my hometown alone, to name but a few things, a multi storey car park was built in 2020. A total blot on the landscape that was not needed nor asked for. Not many people have parked their cars there, since its completion, although it has proven a hit among local skateboarders! Barely a mile away, a cycling lane along the Bristol Road was painted and with around 100 safety bollards put in place along the road, stretching 300-400 yards. Again, not needed nor asked for as an existing cycling lane within very close proximity was already in place. This project was scrapped with the painted lines and bollards removed after barely 9 months. So much money wasted and probably no one held to account either. There are countless examples like this in just about every town and city across the land.

We are not to blame for institutional Police and local Authority failings spanning decades in regards to the thousands of young women and girls, predominantly from the forgotten, former mill towns and cities of Lancashire and Yorkshire, who were left at the mercy of grooming gangs made up mainly of men of North Pakistani origin. Much of the same can be said for those survivors who were also let down terribly after suffering at the hands of Clergy of all denominations and by prominent and influential figures in showbusiness and politics - Most notably, Jimmy Savile. Callous men who were literally given free reign to carry out their evil and wicked crimes in various institutions such as schools and hospitals for many years.

We are not to blame for the appalling and avoidable disasters involving Aircraft and Railways over the years, and the disasters of Aberfan, South Wales, (Spoil tip landslide, destroying school and homes - 1966) Valley Parade Stadium, Bradford, (Terrace blaze - 1985) Hillsborough Stadium, Sheffield (Liverpool fans penned in and crushed against high fences - 1989) and the Grenfell Tower, London. (High Rise, Tower block blaze caused by flammable cladding - 2017)

We are not to blame for high levels of social breakdown and crimes in some of our towns and cities. And with the ever rising

Paul Treacy

rates of teenage pregnancies, absent fathers and abortions.....I could go on and on and on. Although this Subchapter has been called England's Grim Underbelly, it is fair to say that the good folk of Scotland, Wales and Northern Ireland have also been let down many times within their own borders by their own Governments and in so many ways as well as by those within the corridors of Westminster.

'Take pride in knowing that your struggle will play the biggest role in your purpose.' - Marcus Rashford. (This quote is inscribed on his famous Manchester mural as mentioned earlier.)

Why Do You Act The Way You Do??

I bet your parents wished they never had you.
You rub people up the wrong way.
Talking to yourself is the first sign of madness.
You do yourself no favours by acting up this way.
You need your head examined.
What is your major malfunction??
You're about as useful as a chocolate teapot.
One born like you every minute!
You should be ashamed of yourself.
You are really beginning to wind me up!

These are some of the more milder things that I have had said to me from the age of 5 years old, onwards. In some instances, from people who really should have known better. I have had to watch and grin and bear it, as many of my peers have progressed through life and get ahead more whilst I could only get so far. This notion, that I seem to 'rub people up the wrong way' because of my traits and how I handle certain matters is one that I have heard so many times through the years.

Hand on heart, though I am far from perfect and far from angelic in some instances which I will admit to, I do my utmost to treat people the way that I too, would wish to be treated, regardless of anyone's ethnicity, religion or status. I am often misunderstood, pure and simple. The way certain people react towards those with hidden disabilities can well and truly bring out the very worst in a person's nature - And even among generally easy going folk, who, just like me, find racism, sexism and prejudices towards people with physical disabilities as completely abhorrent and unacceptable.

I have met people who I have had so much in common with: they may support the same sports teams as me, enjoy the same tastes in music, movies, and various other subjects - But who still don't take to me kindly, even though we would probably be good friends had I not been on the spectrum. If you the reader, were to introduce someone like me to 5 of your best friends in a bar or cafe, the chances are that at least one of your friends will begin to feel uncomfortable, start to fidget and then make excuses that they have to leave after 15-20 minutes.

Many young men and women on the spectrum will know that horribly sinking feeling all too well when trying to meet and/or being introduced to, new people and are eager to feel accepted and valued. We certainly don't deserve this and wish for others to accept us as for who we are. Over the years, I have faced unpleasant and awkward scenarios of many kinds and have had to turn down invitations to parties, social gatherings and numerous other events as I knew that there would be a minority there who had a less than rosy view of me. (I have never once attended any works Christmas dinner/party for example.)

Much of mainstream society needs to realise that we are not 'odd' or 'strange' in any way: it is that our brains are wired differently. Why this is the case still remains a mystery. We think and act in ways which to us, are as natural as breathing but are totally baffling to others. To date, none of the greatest Doctors and brain experts have ever been able to fully explain as to why and how Autism occurs. Even at our youngest years we gain many interests and think differently about so many things.

While most boys back in my day would dream about scoring the winning goal in an FA Cup Final or becoming a Formula 1 Racing legend, I was, among my many other interests, hugely fixated on the actual meaning of life and asking as to why we are all actually here from the moment I was told I narrowly escaped death as a Baby and the subject was a permanent fixture in my mind. Just what would I have seen and experienced if I had died? Would I have gone to Heaven? Would I be reincarnated? Or would it be a never ending, dreamless sleep? I read about other faiths. I also read, about the theories of the Big Bang and evolution but was never fully convinced, especially with the theory that human beings, homo sapiens, slowly evolved from the apes over tens of thousands of years.

I will not delve deeply into the theory of evolution that is firmly believed by so many but put simply: There is no God or supreme being/s, there is no purpose to anything, no real meaning, no right and wrong. You live your life, reach up to 80 years if you're lucky enough, you die.....And that's basically it. I knew only the basics about Christianity and the Bible before the age of 15. A creator God seemed far more credible to me personally. There is so much design evident throughout our Universe, the Solar System, this Earth, trees, plants, animals and creatures of every kind and of course, human beings. Maybe a spiritual dimension outside of time, space and matter as the Bible says, is actually possible?

Watching the films 'Flatliners' and then 'Ghost' with the latter, starring Patrick Swayze, during my teenage years, really took my interest in the subject of an afterlife to a whole new level. I can still remember shaking in fright as the souls of the hitman who killed Sam (Swayze) and later his so called friend who paid the hitman to kill him, were grabbed by blackened, demonic beings and dragged away to Hell, moments after they died in separate accidents. Even though I was used to watching horror movie characters like Freddy Krueger, it shook me to the core. I really hoped I would not end up in that terrible place and was eager to find out how to avoid going there.

Paul Treacy

Just by chance, shortly after, I found a book that was tucked away in a drawer at home: Power for Living by Jamie Buckingham. It featured some famous names like the singer Cliff Richard and explained Christianity step by step and I found it truly fascinating. What Jesus said and the way he treated others really touched my heart. He spoke the most amazing sermons and parables and of peace and the promise of eternal life. Surely an everyday Carpenter from First Century, Roman occupied Palestine, couldn't just conjure such things up?? He surely had to be who he said he was: The Son of God. I gave my life to Jesus in that Warm Summer of 1992. There would be many challenges and setbacks to come for me over the years. Though I have been let down in many ways and by many people in the near 30 years since, the good Lord has never, ever, let me down.

Jesus and The Marginalised

After being baptised in the Jordan River by John the Baptist and then filled with the Holy Spirit aged 30, Jesus revealed to the world who he really was: The promised Messiah - As foretold through the ages. John the Baptist, who had never previously met Jesus in person until that very moment he showed up to be baptised, knew right there and then, who he was.

Jesus travelled throughout much of the Holy Land and spent a great deal of time with people who were downtrodden and despised by much of regular society at that time: The lame, sick, disabled, prostitutes, beggars and drunkards. Jesus treated such people no less differently, giving them his love and compassion and even ate with them.

This was noticed by the Pharisees who were disgusted and outraged by his actions. But Jesus was undeterred by these hypocrites and spoke about them at great length throughout the entire Chapter of Matthew 23.

[1] Then spake Jesus to the multitude, and to his disciples,

[2] Saying The scribes and the Pharisees sit in Moses' seat:

[3] All therefore whatsoever they bid you observe, that observe and do; but do not ye after their works: for they say, and do not.

[4] For they bind heavy burdens and grievous to be borne, and lay them on men's shoulders; but they themselves will not move them with one of their fingers.

⁵ But all their works they do for to be seen of men: they make broad their phylacteries, and enlarge the borders of their garments,

⁶ And love the uppermost rooms at feasts, and the chief seats in the synagogues,

⁷ And greetings in the markets, and to be called of men, Rabbi, Rabbi.

⁸ But be not ye called Rabbi: for one is your Master, even Christ; and all ye are brethren.

⁹ And call no man your father upon the earth: for one is your Father, which is in heaven.

¹⁰ Neither be ye called masters: for one is your Master, even Christ.

¹¹ But he that is greatest among you shall be your servant.

¹² And whosoever shall exalt himself shall be abased; and he that shall humble himself shall be exalted.

¹³ But woe unto you, scribes and Pharisees, hypocrites! for ye shut up the kingdom of heaven against men: for ye neither go in yourselves, neither suffer ye them that are entering to go in.

¹⁴ Woe unto you, scribes and Pharisees, hypocrites! for ye devour widows' houses, and for a pretence make long prayer: therefore ye shall receive the greater damnation.

¹⁵ Woe unto you, scribes and Pharisees, hypocrites! for ye compass sea and land to make one proselyte, and when he is made, ye make him twofold more the child of hell than yourselves.

¹⁶ Woe unto you, ye blind guides, which say, Whosoever shall swear by the temple, it is nothing; but whosoever shall swear by the gold of the temple, he is a debtor!

¹⁷ Ye fools and blind: for whether is greater, the gold, or the temple that sanctifieth the gold?

¹⁸ And, Whosoever shall swear by the altar, it is nothing; but whosoever sweareth by the gift that is upon it, he is guilty.

¹⁹ Ye fools and blind: for whether is greater, the gift, or the altar that sanctifieth the gift?

[20] Whoso therefore shall swear by the altar, sweareth by it, and by all things thereon.

[21] And whoso shall swear by the temple, sweareth by it, and by him that dwelleth therein.

[22] And he that shall swear by heaven, sweareth by the throne of God, and by him that sitteth thereon.

[23] Woe unto you, scribes and Pharisees, hypocrites! for ye pay tithe of mint and anise and cummin, and have omitted the weightier matters of the law, judgment, mercy, and faith: these ought ye to have done, and not to leave the other undone.

[24] Ye blind guides, which strain at a gnat, and swallow a camel.

[25] Woe unto you, scribes and Pharisees, hypocrites! for ye make clean the outside of the cup and of the platter, but within they are full of extortion and excess.

[26] Thou blind Pharisee, cleanse first that which is within the cup and platter, that the outside of them may be clean also.

[27] Woe unto you, scribes and Pharisees, hypocrites! for ye are like unto whited sepulchres, which indeed appear beautiful outward, but are within full of dead men's bones, and of all uncleanness.

[28] Even so ye also outwardly appear righteous unto men, but within ye are full of hypocrisy and iniquity.

[29] Woe unto you, scribes and Pharisees, hypocrites! because ye build the tombs of the prophets, and garnish the sepulchres of the righteous,

[30] And say, If we had been in the days of our fathers, we would not have been partakers with them in the blood of the prophets.

[31] Wherefore ye be witnesses unto yourselves, that ye are the children of them which killed the prophets.

[32] Fill ye up then the measure of your fathers.

[33] Ye serpents, ye generation of vipers, how can ye escape the damnation of hell?

[34] Wherefore, behold, I send unto you prophets, and wise men, and scribes: and some of them ye shall kill and crucify; and some

of them shall ye scourge in your synagogues, and persecute them from city to city:

[35] That upon you may come all the righteous blood shed upon the earth, from the blood of righteous Abel unto the blood of Zacharias son of Barachias, whom ye slew between the temple and the altar.

[36] Verily I say unto you, All these things shall come upon this generation.

[37] O Jerusalem, Jerusalem, thou that killest the prophets, and stonest them which are sent unto thee, how often would I have gathered thy children together, even as a hen gathereth her chickens under her wings, and ye would not!

[38] Behold, your house is left unto you desolate.

[39] For I say unto you, Ye shall not see me henceforth, till ye shall say, Blessed is he that cometh in the name of the Lord.

The Pharisees, the so called 'holy men' were in essence, an out of touch, inward looking 'old boys network' who seemed to be more interested in their wealth and privilege, while trying to make themselves look virtuous, rather than properly serving God and helping hard up, everyday people whom they heckled on a regular basis. Notice the passion and anger in the way Jesus lays into these Pharisees throughout the chapter. (Jesus certainly did not condone the lifestyles of some of those he met and ate with but always tried to show them the errors of their ways.) Those who point the longest and shout the loudest at those they deemed to be beneath them are always the biggest hypocrites.

There are numerous reasons as to why I decided to include the entire chapter of Matthew 23. So many of my fellow Britons have never read so much as ten verses of the Good Book, let alone an entire Biblical chapter before. In John 15: 18,19 he says "If the world hate you, ye know that it hated me before it hated you. If ye were of the world, the world would love his own: but because ye are not of the world, but I have chosen you out of the world, therefore the world hateth you." This is something that I can personally relate to a great deal.

Jesus himself never owned a house, never had any possessions or titles to his name. He went on to heal the sick and cure illnesses of all kinds with miracles and tell the most truly thought provoking, amazing and heart-warming parables. Many people turned away from their sinful and destructive lifestyles after meeting him and followed him.

Aged 33, he was later betrayed by one of his disciples, Judas Iscariot, for 30 pieces of silver, then later handed over to the Roman authorities, whose Judean Governor, Pontius Pilate, caved in to a raging mob, demanding him to be crucified, which at first he refused then later granted. The beaten and horrendously scourged Jesus had a crown of thorns placed upon his head and given a robe in a mocking fashion, was then made to carry his own cross and crucified at a hilltop outside Jerusalem, known as Golgotha (The Skull) in between two thieves. The act of crucifixion itself, even though many centuries old, is still among the most slowest and agonising of executions ever devised by man. If a man has not been too badly beaten and/or starved prior to crucifixion, he can live for over 48 hours nailed to a cross until he dies.

After being laid to rest in a tomb, he rose again on the third day, conquering death and was seen by many hundreds of people before ascending to Heaven and sending the Holy Spirit down. He truly was the Son of God and changed the course of human history forever, changing the lives of so many millions of people from all cultures and walks of life, throughout the ages. No one man has shaped history more.

'Now when the centurion, and they that were with
him, watching Jesus, saw the earthquake, and those
things that were done, they feared greatly, saying,
Truly this was the Son of God.' Matthew 27:54

Many Snakes, Few Ladders

Imagine if you will, it is the morning of Christmas Day. You unwrap a present which happens to be a Snakes and Ladders board game. You mentioned to your Spouse or close relative that you enjoyed playing that game as a child with your siblings and parents on rainy weekends. The box looks pretty plain and featureless but you don't really think much of it until you take the folded board out, place it upon the table and open it up.

To your utter shock, it is unlike any Snakes and Ladders board that you have ever seen before. The snakes heavily outnumber the ladders. And the 3 ladders that are on the board are really short. You crack on and try to play the game but after nearly 2 very frustrating hours, with neither of you making any real progress, you both decide to put the game away - for good. It then gets left to gather dust on top of the wardrobe.

Now imagine if you will.... If your very LIFE was similar to that particular board game! You play by the rules and keep on trying your best but to no avail and with constant frustration. But, just like the board game, the fact that where you want to get to and what you wish to achieve is not totally impossible, keeps driving you on. This is the situation that so many people with hidden disabilities find themselves in while trying to progress through every aspect of their lives but who continually face setbacks and pitfalls that are not of their own making.

I know only too well how this feels. You desperately want to say and do the right thing in order to get ahead and make the very best and right impression but it is often so much tougher than it is for most other regular people. You can begin to notice that others start to become annoyed with you, their body language is totally negative and that many will not take you seriously. Some will mock and humiliate you while insisting that you only have yourself to blame. And so it goes on.

Autistic people are often very highly talented people and with a whole abundance of skills. But these are often overlooked because of societal prejudice and institutional, systemic failings that keep so many of us downtrodden and unable to fulfil our full potential - In countless cases, for life.

If there were more greater understanding, awareness, acceptance and the chances for more better investment and opportunities, starting from the earliest primary school years, hundreds of thousands of people the world over could live happier and more prosperous lives while also contributing Billions to their national economy every year.

To date, I have always had a clean driving licence, have no criminal record and have never once been arrested. My currently teenage son has not been in trouble with the law either. (Hope it stays that way.) Yet even still, so many people see me negatively, even though my Autism does not define me. Politicians and prominent, business and finance leaders can play a huge part in making much needed reforms, which I will discuss more further on.

Please Don't Worry – They Don't Bite

"You need not worry. They're a really friendly bunch of people."

"There are people from all walks of life who worship here. We have students who have come here to study from all over the world. And we have Caribbean and Polish families among us."

"You have Autism? Well, we have a lad here with Downs Syndrome and another who is nearly deaf. You'll fit in just great."

These may be among some of the typical kinds of things that someone on the Autism Spectrum might hear from a friend or someone who is trying to encourage them to attend their local Church. The individual in question may already be a Christian. S/he may be 'on the fence' as it were and possibly curious to know more - Or they may even be a staunch atheist.

Encouraging people with hidden disabilities to come along to Church can be a tough task in itself. What is even tougher is trying to encourage them to continue coming along - Even for some committed, Autistic Christians for a whole variety of reasons.

Many people on the Autism Spectrum struggle terribly in social situations, especially in regards to meeting new people. The overwhelming majority will have faced bullying at school, at home, in the streets and at work, if they have ever been employed at all. Due to this, many will experience low self-esteem and self-worth.

(A large percentage will have endured physical and sexual abuse in childhood years.)

Fidgeting, routine and in some cases, ritualistic, 'stimming' behaviour are often common factors as they are coping mechanisms when they find themselves in awkward and uncomfortable situations. Very sadly, a lot of people in society perceive and label this display of behaviour as people being 'disrespectful' and 'difficult' though this is certainly far from the case. They - We - DO want to make a good impression and to fit in but certain tasks that so many people take for granted such as regular eye contact, keeping attentive & trying to cease fidgeting/stimming are extremely difficult for many of us. The view from mainstream society is that Autistic people should simply stop being 'annoying': to try and snap out of it and make more of an effort.

This 'make more of an effort' mindset, while to some may be said with the best of intentions, is actually deeply damaging to both us and to our families.

Statistics have shown that rates of anxiety, depression, self harm & very sadly, suicides, are far higher among Autistic people than among the general population. Along with mental health struggles, unemployment, poverty & poor health rates are also typically higher. Average life expectancy rates are usually lower.

It seems that even many ex-convicts here in Britain are offered more opportunities in bettering their lives than people like me. Now please don't get me wrong: It is good when someone is given another chance and for the most part, depending on the nature of the man's conviction, I am usually fully supportive of that. However, my own 'crime' was to be born with a neurological condition.

It is with this in mind that I will give you a quick snapshot of how much of my own life has fared so far, my first 35 years from 1976 to 2012, to let you understand what I have been through: The setbacks, rampant discrimination and the many lose-lose situations forced upon me, that have shaped my life, along the way.

Some may read through the section about my life & conclude that I am 'partly to blame' in all of this. But, I would really love to know how they would have done things so differently while being under the exact, same circumstances.

You will see that I had the misfortune of having to deal with some very manipulating & cowardly people, abusing their positions that they were completely unfit for - While growing up in an uncompromising era where scapegoating established minorities & working class youth was the norm - Which was aided and abetted by much of the repugnant, mainstream media at the time.

PART TWO

Just An Everyday Guy

I am just an everyday guy from Wiltshire: the beautiful English County which is the home of Stonehenge and the Avebury stone circles. And also the County where notable figures ranging from Sir Christopher Wren, the architect of St Paul's Cathedral in London to Diana Dors the actress to 1960s chart toppers, Dave Dee, Dozy, Beaky, Mick and Tich, all come from. (Sir Christopher Wren also designed much of Central London after the Great Fire of 1666.)

If you were to pass me in the street prior to me writing this book, you wouldn't give me a second glance. There are no airs and graces with me. I treat people the way that I too, wish to be treated. I am really into my sports, like most regular guys here. Love Soccer, Rugby, Formula 1 and Boxing, though was never really any good at playing soccer and rugby myself. I used to regularly play the genteel game of Bowls at my local Club but, at this time of writing, it has been a while since I last played it. I have never had an allegiance to any political party. My views then as now, vary, depending on the subject matter. I am probably the most unlikeliest of Christian book authors.....possibly ever! I grew up on a typical, English council estate during the 1980s.

(My ancestor just so happens to be William De Tracy: One of the Knights who slayed the then, Archbishop of Canterbury, Thomas Beckett, during the 12th Century after he and his fellow Knights mistakenly believed King Henry II, wished to have him killed.)

I can fully well relate to well known British TV figures who hail from my area such as Billie Piper from Swindon and siblings Daisy May Cooper and Charlie Cooper from Cirencester – And like me, also hail from humble beginnings. Where I was born, where I grew up, from 1978 onwards, both of the schools I attended and the streets where I played and whizzed around on my bikes: the huge majority of my childhood years, were all within less than a 2 mile radius. The mock tudor designed hospital where I was born could be seen from the upper half of the street where I lived before it was demolished, somewhere around 1990 time. From my bedroom window, I could see the spire of the nearest and largest Church in my area: St Paul's Church. Thus, thoughts of God were of regular occurrence for me. Because of both the nearest Church and my School being called St Paul's, the area of Chippenham where I grew up in was often, jokingly, given the unofficial name of St Pauls – However, this was usually not actually a term of endearment as nearby Bristol has an area called St Pauls: an area with a large, Caribbean community, which was often mentioned on the local news throughout much of the 1980s and 1990s….And nearly always for the wrong reasons.

Most of the neighbours, were good, down to earth people: the backbone of Britain. Many of whom were employed at the Westinghouse, Railway Brake and Signal Company, which was the main employer among Chippenham folk during that time. Although both my parents often attended Church in their earlier years, I only ever attended Church on special occasions during mine. Dad was raised a Catholic and Mum a Protestant but thankfully it was never an issue among our families as it may have been in other areas such as Northern Ireland, for example. My Liberal leaning parents always said they would respect whatever I decided or not to believe in, though the subject of Faith very rarely got mentioned. As far as I knew, virtually no one regularly attended Church in the area I grew up: Not even the older men who served in the World Wars and those who also served in the military over in India and other faraway areas during the years of the British Empire. 'Religion and all that' was deemed old fashioned among the young and was usually the subject of ridicule in films and plays such as Monty Phython's infamous, 'The Life of Brian.'

For most British youth and older children from the 1950s onwards, music, fashion and socialising was among the core centre of our lives. For many of the Chippenham youth during this era, the 'Temple' as it were, was the Goldiggers nightclub, which for a while was owned and sometimes frequented by the Virgin Company tycoon, Richard Branson. Bands like The Jam, The Culture Club and The Boomtown Rats performed there during its heyday and my Dad attended numerous gigs and events there. (Unfortunately, its best days were already over by the time I was old enough to go there myself at weekends.) The club has since been demolished. It must be said that there was rarely a dull moment while growing up during the 1980s.

Even during that decade, trends, fashions and ideas came and went fairly fast. And despite the 'Cold War' with American and Soviet Union tensions becoming a regular feature on our news screens, I was full of optimism for the future, regularly dreaming of life as a grown up Man and the many golden opportunities that laid ahead once I worked hard, proved my worth and tried my best in every aspect of life.

Unfortunately, as I was to learn the very hard way, this was all an illusion because I was often seen as being 'inferior' and 'retarded' by many over the coming years. And the wheels were to soon fall off - Very fast.

Earliest years.

I was born in December 1976 in my hometown of Chippenham in the County of Wiltshire in southern England, located 100 miles to the West of London. My Father was from a large, Irish Catholic family and grew up in the area. He was a well known local builder who was a popular figure in the local pubs and social clubs. He attended some of the most iconic rock concerts in England and in the area during his earlier years. Among his friends were some of Chippenham's most liveliest characters, including people from Asian and Caribbean backgrounds and with some of them often visiting our house, which wasn't a common sight in less urban areas back in those days. Even before I was legally old enough to have my first pint at eighteen, I had probably stepped foot into at least 200 pubs across the country, spanning from Plymouth in Devonshire, right the way up to the Scottish town of Peterhead in Aberdeenshire. (We even once visited the famous Woolpack pub in West Yorkshire which features in the Emmerdale soap series.) Dad's work sometimes took him as far as Holland and what was then known as West Germany. Thousands of British tradesmen worked over in continental Europe in the late 1970s to the mid 1980s because of the great rates of pay on offer and lack of work for many in some parts of Britain during this time. A very popular TV comedy/drama called 'Auf Weidersehen Pet', about the lives of such men working overseas, was even made.

My Mother was originally from the 'Granite City' of Aberdeen in Scotland and for a while, lived in West Germany where her own Mother was from before moving to England. Both my parents had been separated from previous marriages. They met at The Five Alls pub, now a Chinese restaurant, where Mum was doing part time bar work. Dad already had a son and daughter. Mum already had a son.

During the first few weeks of my life, I was very close to death after struggling with breathing difficulties. The year of 1976 in Britain had a record breaking hot Summer followed later by a bitterly cold Winter. The first house I lived at in the town of Corsham had dampness within and it is strongly believed to have caused my very early health problems. I spent a great deal of time in an incubator at Bath Royal United Hospital. My parents were told that my chances of survival were slim and that I would require a lot of care if I did survive as I would be very frail.

Thankfully, neither situation occurred, though it would appear that I wasn't completely unscathed. My parents were greatly relieved.

We later moved 5 miles from our house in Corsham to a three bedroom house in Chippenham and shortly after, my full blooded sibling, Matthew, was born in 1979. But even from my very earliest years, I knew - As did everyone else - That I was somewhat 'different' from all the other children in the neighbourhood.

I was often left out when local kids were out playing and I could never really understand why. For every Birthday Party I was invited to, Matthew was invited to 5-6 more. And he was always far more popular.

Despite the political, social and economic turmoil around the time of my earlier years and with the exception of two unpleasant accidents with one of them requiring stitches to my face, the first 9-10 years of my life were reasonable enough. We usually had 1-2 annual holidays, mainly on the English south coast in Devonshire, Dorset and the Isle of Wight in particular, where we have relations. We visited Scotland twice and Germany during my childhood years too. My hometown of Chippenham was then voted as one of Britain's finest towns. It was a smaller but nicer place at the time. The town's population has trebled since my birth. (In 2021, Chippenham surpassed the City of Salisbury as the being the second most populated urban area of the County of Wiltshire.) Dad was out a great deal, as were my brothers. I would usually be at home with Mum and with my nose in a book.

My young mind was full of many dreams. I was fascinated with Nature, Science, Dinosaurs, Aviation and countless events through History. I loved flicking through World atlases, studying the Continents, Countries and Oceans. I knew the capital cities of countless nations and was familiar with many national flags.

Throughout most of the 1980s, my Primary school was then the most modern in town. All the classrooms were open plan and there was even a small, swimming pool on the campus. We didn't even have to wear uniforms either.

With the exception of the Headmaster, as Headteachers were then known and a short term, supply teacher, all the teachers were aging ladies. If you are familiar with the prim and proper, Hyacinth Bucket (pronounced 'Bouquet' on her insistence) from the classic, British sitcom, 'Keeping up Appearances' then you will realise that this stereotype was typical of so many well to do Ladies during the late 20th century. The then Prime Minister, Margaret Thatcher, being among the most famous example.

All the teachers were very 'Hyacinth' in their ways. Most were strict and although they all meant well, they were not particularly suitable and too old fashioned for a modern school in a predominantly working class area of Chippenham, dealing with hyperactive, Council Estate kids raised on a hardcore diet of pop music, soccer, The A Team & Thundercats.

The Headmaster would sometimes take over a class when a regular teacher was away. In one class he was reminiscing about his own childhood and how he enjoyed reading Biggles and The Famous Five. He asked what books and films we enjoyed.

In my typical fashion, I blurted out that I enjoyed watching films with Arnold Schwarzenegger in them. He wasn't familiar with who he was. I explained in the typical & hilarious Wiltshire way that he was a 'gert' big guy with massive muscles & I enjoyed watching The Terminator, Predator and The Running Man which he starred in. And yeah, I'm was not actually supposed to watch them as I was not old enough but hey, all kids watch them anyway.

He was totally shocked by what I said as were the class. I often spoke my mind which often got me into trouble. I watched plenty of these kinds of films in younger years, though the earlier James Bond films were a favourite of mine and watched one at least every other week.

The teachers could never figure me out and I was regularly referred to as being a difficult daydreamer. During my earlier years, I was often the joker of the pack both at school and at play with the few I managed to make friends with at the time and loved making people laugh with my daft stories, my impressions of famous people and with the various British and various, other accents that I could pull off. I reached the highest level in reading. I read so many books. But despite this, I always had bad school reports and was often labelled as being naughty and disruptive. It was always tough to try and make new friends. Sometimes, my mind went into overdrive. At one stage, the class were once asked to draw a poster to highlight road safety and to be viewed by the staff of Hewitts, a then local car dealership in the town. I decided to 'spice up' my drawing with helicopters firing rockets and with bazookas and guns being fired from vans, cars and motorbikes. This, after a long weekend being glued to watching action-adventure programmes like The A-Team, Knight Rider and Street Hawk! I presented my drawing to the teacher, absolutely beaming with pride but it was met with utter horror. I was very upset when she did not approve of it as to me, I felt that I had drawn a masterpiece and genuinely could not see what the problem was.

I always loved the school trips out of Chippenham, whether it was to Ismbard Kingdom Brunel's famous, SS Great Britain ship in Bristol or to the Planetarium (Observatory) in London. I truly enjoyed learning new things - And still do. Going somewhere different was always such an exciting experience for me at that age.

As I now begin to get older, I can begin to understand my primary school teachers and the Headmaster more. They were from a bygone era and grew up during the onset of the Second World War. They would have all had their lives turned upside down for years, not knowing at the time what the future held and may very well have had friends and family members who would have went on to fight in Europe and possibly beyond in North Africa and the jungles of Burma (as Myanmar was then known) with some possibly never returning home. As far as I am aware, they all held strong Christian beliefs and although it didn't often feel like it at times back in the day, deep down, they genuinely cared for all the children they taught. Hence, why my reading abilities were of such of good standard by the time I left there. We often had assemblies where we sang hymns, albeit grudgingly, and a local Vicar would regularly come to talk to us, usually on Friday afternoons.

Autism awareness was barely heard of at the time. My traits were always dismissed as bad behaviour. Always. In fact the only time I had even heard of Autism in my entire childhood years was in the case of Stephen Wiltshire, who was in the more rare 'Sauvant' category. The then teenager from London could look at a city landscape for just a few minutes then paint it in absolute fine detail, elsewhere. He was taken to New York City and the paintings he done were absolutely astonishing.

The 'Rainman' film starring Dustin Hoffman as a Autistic Sauvant and Co starring Tom Cruise, came out in the late 1980s but I never seen it until over 20 years later. Unfortunately, many people who have watched Rainman still think this portrayal is typical of the entire Autism Spectrum.

This Isn't Fair!

Before and during the lovely Summer of 1988, I held huge hopes for life at secondary school. Our primary school class visited there for a few days shortly before we left there for good. Many of the teachers were more around my parents age and seemed more liberal in their ways. However, much to my dismay, most of the following 5 years would prove to be a really horrible time there for me.

Many teachers were reasonable enough and to be fair, some of them were truly great, including the three different tutors I had, during those years. However, there was a culture where the children from more affluent backgrounds, whatever their abilities, were put on a pedestal and given more favourable treatment. I completely refused to believe that anyone I went to school with, especially those from a more affluent background, were somehow 'better' and more 'superior' to me. It used to really annoy me having to continually being told that they were in effect, literally the best thing since sliced bread – And having to watch them being continually being presented awards with and certificates during assemblies, over and over – And in many cases, for activities for which I was not given the chance to participate in. It eventually got to the stage where I simply refused to clap them when they were presented with awards. And can you truly blame me??

The school campus was spread over a large area and sometimes it just wasn't possible to get from one opposite end to the other in the expected 5 minute timeframe. I was in a fair few classes during those years where lessons were dumbed down to a 9-11 year olds level of teaching. I knew that such lessons would never allow for me to progress but what exactly could I do? I knew in my heart of hearts that I should not have been in such classes. No point mentioning it to my parents I thought as they would probably insist that the teachers knew best. Some lessons were completely boring and fruitless, while others were downright difficult. I did not ever like to ask for help if I ever got stuck with anything, else I would risk the wrath of being bullied and humiliated. Instead, I would take a wild guess with any question/s and just hope for the best.

On one particular term in English, we had to write an essay about our favourite Soap Opera. Here was the problem - I didn't have one! I never watched Emmerdale, Brookside or 'Corrie' - as we Brits often refer to Coronation Street. In the end, I opted to watch Eastenders and had a very miserable time trying to learn all the names of the characters and the current plot. There was a stigma that everyone from a working-class background watched the soaps.

There were a small hardcore there who really had it in for me and who would think nothing of shouting and humiliating me in front of a full class which was a totally crushing experience. My older brother from my Dad's first marriage had already been and gone when I arrived at secondary school. He had a bit of a reputation during his own years and I was sometimes reminded of this.

These kind of teachers would fan the flames for kids to pick on one another and to then normalise it as being part and parcel of life. Struggling kids and those with learning difficulties were generally seen as being weak.

Although I left primary school as being among the best readers and who could spell the vast majority of words perfectly, I ended up in the lowest sets for English and various other subjects. I won a Governors Award in Science but got sneered at and told it was only given on 'sympathy.' (The term 'political correctness' had not been coined at the time.)

Basically, a minority of working-class kids were given awards so that their parents and the more left leaning teachers didn't complain that only the 'posh' kids kept on winning the awards all the time. Any progress I was making at the time just didn't feel like progress at all in the end.

During my early to mid-teens, I sometimes contemplated suicide as I felt I was just no good and a burden to my family. My self-esteem and self-worth was almost non-existent. I had huge aspirations to go to college and hopefully one day work for Future Publishing in Bath. They published the 'Sega Power' computer games magazine that I bought on a regular basis. Then one day I thought - Forget it mate - it will never happen.

Britain, during the early 1990's, was a very different place. Institutional racism and sexism was still very much intact. Working-class youth were demonised on an almost daily basis by much of the Mainstream Media with phrases like 'The ecstasy generation' and 'Acid house zombies' often doing the rounds.

All this, combined with a looming recession made for a very toxic mix. I never took any recreational drugs but was often falsely accused of taking them. The News often shown illegal raves being broken up, footage of 'joy riding' taking place and regular programmes about the drunken and debauched antics of young, British holiday makers across the Mediterranean from Ibiza to Cyprus. In previous years, Britain seen the subcultures of Teddy Boys, Mods and Rockers, Punks and Skinheads, all of whom had their fair share of bad press, but now it seemed as if the majority of under 25s everywhere during 1988-1995 were being tarred as being untrustworthy 'wrong uns.'

As this was an era before the launch of the Internet, most of the general public took what was being said as being gospel truth - That this new generation was saturated with lazy, drug fuelled monsters who lived for the weekend and were willingly intent on causing misery for others. Many shopkeepers also started to insist that only one child of school age could enter their shop at a time. Something I never seen, prior to 1988.

As I got older and my Autism became more challenging, many more people assumed that I was using recreational drugs. Also, because I was single most of the time as local girls had absolutely no interest in me, some people assumed I was gay. And I would often be called derogatory names.

During the tail end of school life, the fact that I was mainly well behaved and of good character: having a strong work ethic and having a paper round, which I had done in all weathers from Mondays to Saturdays, still did not change the views of some people. It was nigh on impossible for someone like me to make any kind of progress in that kind of unpleasant environment and for my true abilities to flourish. To me, it seemed that those such as myself should 'know our place' - And that is being at or close to, the bottom of the societal ladder.

All of the excitement and energy I had entering secondary school in September 1988 in the firm belief it would be an almighty stepping stone to shaping the rest of my life for the better were long gone by the time I was leaving in May 1993.

And just weeks after the infamous murder of the black London teenager, Stephen Lawrence (with the typical speculation he was a thug who 'lived and died by the sword' - Which was of course, totally untrue) came my last ever day at school. And even on that day, I was granted no dignity as my name was left out of the school yearbook on purpose. The yearbook was little more than a booklet but it still hurt and demoralised me terribly.

Not surprisingly, I left school with very little qualifications. These results were certainly not a true reflection of me and my abilities. I will always firmly believe that I was deliberately set up for failure. Had it not been for the fact that I decided to become a Christian in 1992 after reading 'Power for Living' by Jamie Buckingham then maybe life would have got the better of me. I could have very well have possibly descended into addiction and maybe later go on to take my own life. Would my childhood years have been easier if I were diagnosed with Autism back in those days? Personally, I feel that, because of the way things were back then, probably not. Maybe, things could have possibly been a lot worse. During my entire eleven years of schooling, I was never once suspended or expelled.

Toxic Mid Nineties

Sadly, I was to endure even worse over the next couple of years. I left school unsure as what to do. A career in writing seemed off the cards for me, as I didn't think I was smart enough. I done work experience at the Midland Bank in Malmesbury in June 1992 but got sneered at often and was told that I had no chance in having a career in Banking. So, I gave up that idea too. I made a very ill judged decision to enrol in a sports and leisure course at the local college with a friend. Playing sports was never my speciality, especially with having tree trunk legs! (My legs have nearly always been short for my height for some bizarre reason.) He dropped out just 2 months in and I struggled throughout the rest of the course and was unable to make any proper friendships. I dropped out myself the following Summer.

I started work for the very first time at a local meat processing plant and was hired via an agency but was laid off after just 6 weeks, despite having never received any prior complaints and worked just as hard as everyone else, all while earning around £1.50 an hour less than regular staff. Just days beforehand, my locker was broken into and the contents within were stolen. By the time I had replaced my items and got to the factory floor, I was around 10 minutes late for my shift and this was deemed enough to warrant my dismissal. They called my house which my Dad answered. They simply said they 'will call me again if they ever needed me'. They couldn't bring themselves to say I would not be needed again.

There was to be no sympathy from the Job Centre staff either.

"Well, that's not a very good start, is it??" huffed the frumpy member of staff wearing huge, chunky glasses and who sighed with everything I said. She obviously dismissed what I said about being unfairly laid off as a lie, that I was undoubtedly lazy and workshy and the staff probably thought the same of every single lad under 25 who turned up, down on his luck.

I was then given an almighty form to take home and fill in to claim for welfare. After several totally miserable hours, I sent it off, only for it to be returned by post just days later with many angry looking messages on post-it notes, written in red biro, stating which parts I didn't fill in correctly. Dad asked what the letter was about and I explained it to him as gently as I could. But he lost his rag with me and vowed to find me a job himself. And he did.

About a week later, Dad handed me a piece of scrap paper. A number for a local warehouse. My 7 months there was among one of the most darkest chapters of my life. Once again, I was hired via an agency. The pay was even worse as was my treatment there, much of which cannot be described in this book.

The walk to the warehouse took 45 minutes and I left the house early. On dozens of occasions, even during heavy rain and sub-zero temperatures and usually with about 20 minutes of walking to go, the supervisor would drive past me (and never once stopping to pick me up) often slowing down as he done so before picking up speed again. There is no way I could have driven by a colleague if the roles had been reversed. Even if I was the CEO of a large company and was driving a Rolls Royce, I would have pulled over to pick up one of my workers, walking to work in terrible weather.

I managed to leave in March 1995. It felt like an absolute liberation. The warehouse closed down just a few years later.

The agency regularly phoned me to inform me that I was making great progress and that I would be taken on full time. But this never happened. They called me back the following year and asked if I would like to return. I explained in detail what happened during my truly awful time there but the agency woman tried to play the whole thing down and put a spin on it, patronising me that I needed to 'bear in mind' that the supervisor was often under 'considerable pressure' in his role. Absolute nonsense! I never returned. And I managed to end the conversation without losing my temper.

Worldly Days

Thankfully, I never experienced anything that bad again, though I did have several more bad experiences along the way including another locker break in and theft. Once you get to a certain height and weight, very few people are reluctant to bother you. How I wish I could have been my current 2021 height (6ft) and weight (18.5st) as a teenager in 1994!

From 1995 to 2008, I spent a total of 9 years at a chicken processing plant which used to be based in a nearby Wiltshire village and 3 years at the Dyson, vacuum cleaner plant in Malmesbury. Also done a few other jobs here and there.

Over the years, I was never given the opportunity to climb up the ranks. Although I made some great friends, there was always a minority at all levels that I could just never get on with, no matter how hard I tried to get on with them.

Out of work, I often shown my true colours and tried live the best life I could under my circumstances and with the wages I earned. People often assumed that my Dad paid for my holidays and trips out but I told them I was simply very careful with my money and that they too could do those same kind of things if they really wanted to.

As well as visiting much of Britain and Ireland in my early to mid 20s, I travelled a fair bit of the world, making 3 trips across the Atlantic in under 18 months (Toronto, New York City, Seattle – In that order) and visited much of continental Europe from Madrid

Spain to Moscow Russia. I attended numerous sporting events, mostly soccer, watching both Chippenham Town regularly and my beloved Liverpool FC, (I am a big fan) here and there at one stage. I travelled to Moscow in 2002 to see Liverpool play over there, along with a contingent of just under 800 travelling fans. Visiting Russia was a very unique experience and I visited Red Square on the morning after the game.

Everyone knew I had a brain on me and I could talk about many subjects under the sun. But there was no way I could shake off my love/hate me 'Marmite' tag, no matter how friendly and polite I was. Thankfully, I am far more liked than disliked, compared to my 20th century days.

Since becoming a Christian, I never had any doubts, no matter what life threw at me. My faith was never shaken. But I felt like that I simply didn't fit in when I first tried to visit Church in the mid 90s. Struggling to talk and socialise with others and not realising I was Autistic was very tough. Working in a factory in my late teens while other Christians around my age, who were usually from more affluent, middle class families, were heading for University, made me feel totally inadequate. (Once they reached their mid 20s to early 30s, they would all be guaranteed to have fantastic careers, strong marriages and much recognition from the church, which just wasn't on the cards for me.) It was a double whammy. Most of the churches in town at the time had an average attendance of only around 50 people, most of whom were elderly folk from the suburbs and nearby villages and I felt that no one would understand what everyday life was like for me if I somehow did try to explain it to them.

I always felt like a very huge black cloud loomed over me when others wanted to know more about me and my life. I felt like there was no real possible way that I could truly 'fit in' with the local Christians at that time. Eventually, I became so demoralised by my situation and circumstances that I ceased attending Church services for the huge majority of Sundays, spanning from mid 1996 right up until 2009. (In Britain, only a very small minority of white, working class people attend any place of worship.)

Over those years, I gradually became more worldly like most of my peers and spent most weekends drinking heavily, usually after returning home from soccer matches on Saturday's and was resigned to the notion that I would never get above the 'glass ceiling' that society placed over me. That's just the way it is. Get used to it, I thought.

In the Summer of 2003, my then girlfriend announced that she was pregnant, just weeks after my brother Matthew announced that he was to become a Dad. Although I put on a brave face, I was absolutely terrified on the inside. Over the months, I had succumbed to a deep depression. What on earth had I done?? I always wanted to be a parent but not like this. I was completely unprepared.

Joseph was born on the unique date of April 4 2004 - 04/04/04. An absolutely beautiful boy with a full head of hair. I barely had more than £100 in my bank account at the time and felt like the worst parent ever. I made a solemn vow that he would never end up as a loser like me. I never had any more children and made a promise to never have any more.

Work at the chicken processing plant became more physically demanding. The whole place and culture changed very quickly in a short time. When I first worked there from 1995 to early 1999, the majority of staff were English folk from within an 8 mile radius of Chippenham. Upon my return in late 2002, the majority of staff were Swindon based people of foreign origin.

There were many lovely people among them. Most were originally from nations and cultures where worker exploitation was rife. The firm, which was taken over by another firm during my Dyson years, knew this, and it was the increasing workload and not the foreign staff that made things even more grim. (Just wanted to make that crystal clear.)

I would often return home from work completely exhausted and totally fed up. I would struggle almost daily with regular back pain and numbing migraines. I would be in no mood to play with Joseph or take him to the nearby playground, often going to bed early. Morale at work and home was often low.

This had an impact on my relationship with Joseph's Mother, my fiancé, who I still hoped to Marry. Eventually it became too much and I broke up the relationship, especially as I felt that Joseph would have had a miserable childhood if we both stuck together.

After a year without having a fixed address, I moved into shared accommodation in a squalid place very close to Matthew's house. I 'lived' there for just over 2 years. I let myself go, so to speak and drank even more at weekends. My room was often full of empty beer bottles and cans.

Mental Health Struggles

During the Spring of 2008, it was announced that the chicken processing plant was to close in September that year. Personally, I was relieved. To be honest, I never enjoyed working there. The site has since been demolished, is now a small housing estate and the villagers of Sutton Benger were glad to see it go because of the constant influx of trucks day and night and the vulgar smell that would loom within a half mile radius of the plant, during the height of the Summer.

I had to go to sign on at the local Job centre for the first time in years and on the very same day Joseph started school. After a quick break to the beach town of Southend on Sea in Essex, I returned feeling very confident I would find something new, despite the looming 'credit crunch' recession at the time.

But it wasn't until it was announced that the entire branch of Woolworths stores would close throughout the country in December 2008 with the loss of 30,000 jobs, when I realised just how bad things would actually get.

I kept up my chin up and was confident something would eventually come along my way. Spring 2009 came and went..... Then Summer, then Autumn.....Again, without luck. As the Winter approached, my mental health started to deteriorate and then debts started to rise. Foolishly, I refused to sell my car for nearly 2 years after my redundancy as I kept telling myself I would find another job soon enough and would need to keep hold of it. My redundancy pay was meagre and was soon spent. When you can no longer afford to own a car in an urban area your prospects are diminished to a degree but this increases a great deal in a less urban setting. Add a disability of any kind to that equation and your prospects diminish even further. I felt truly awful when I didn't have any money to be able to buy Joseph so much as a lollipop on a Saturday afternoon when I had him for a few hours. My benefits were soon swallowed up very quickly when I got them.

I tried to keep myself busy and active, doing some voluntary work at a homeless charity called the Doorway Project and attended group sessions at the local Wiltshire Mind, mental health, drop in group in town and had met some wonderful people, some of whom had also hit hard times because of the recession. This helped enormously during some very challenging times and broadened my understanding of mental health issues.

However, the sympathy that some people initially had for me after my redundancy, 12 months previously, slowly began to fizzle away. I then started to receive some fairly unpleasant messages on my Facebook page.

"What?? You STILL haven't found a job yet??."

"You're simply not trying hard enough."

"If I was in your position, what I would do is...."

"You're not setting a good example to your boy by being a layabout."

These are some of the typical kinds of ignorant messages I received by certain 'friends' on the platform over the following years. I only followed some of them due to the fact they were friends of other people in my family. Numerous people began to question me and unfollowed me on the platform during the early 2010's. (Am no longer on the platform and am the more happier for it.) Even an innocuous message like simply saying I fed some stale bread to the ducks on the river would prompt such messages. Attitudes were still hardened among people, even after my 2010 Autism diagnosis. Thankfully, no one in my family were ever like this. During these challenging times, day to day life would often be made tougher with regular lack of sleep, extreme anxiety and occasional dizziness, hampering my daily, quality of life. (My mental health struggles were a common occurrence throughout just about all of my teenage years. Getting help for such struggles in less urban areas were pretty much non existent back then.)

I gained solace by regularly returning to Church for the first time in years after enrolling in an 'Alpha Course' and meeting some lovely and supportive people. I even enrolled in the similar, 'Christianity Explored' course shortly after. One chap in particular, Keith Oliver, who represented Great Britain in Skiing in his younger years during the 1970s was a like a Father figure and he helped me to gain a confidence that I never previously had.

On my 33rd Birthday of all days, things started picking up. I moved into my own flat just outside Chippenham Town centre for the first time via a mental health support scheme and lived there for nearly 5 years. In November 2010, I was baptised at Station Hill Baptist Church, Chippenham.

Good Causes and Challenges Ahead

During 2011, I along with a few others, helped set up an organisation called HEALS - Help, Encouragement And Local Support. (The word Encouragement was later replaced with Empowerment.) This group, based in historic Malmesbury, 10 miles north of Chippenham, helped many local people via a whole variety of ways. Unsurprisingly, not everyone was warm to the idea of the organisation at first in the firm belief that it just simply wasn't needed there. However, that soon began to change once local church leaders and local newspapers gave us their full backing. I ran the Twitter page and was the person who came up with the HEALS sunshine logo. The charity has since, entered its 10th anniversary and has achieved some incredibly amazing things during that time. We only anticipated that it would probably reach 3 years.

I went to Malmesbury as often as I could for meetings and social events, even going further ahead to Clerkenwell in London to a charity exhibition. (HEALS won several awards including 2nd place in the local charity category at the 2014 Wiltshire Life Magazine Awards in Marlborough.) We held a memorable, fundraising dinner event and auction at an exclusive hotel in Cardiff, South Wales and the former Everton FC and Wales goalkeeper, Neville Southall, was our guest of honour. A truly fantastic chap - And that's coming from a fan of the Red half of Merseyside!

During the height of the London 2012 Olympics, the Wiltshire Mind charity, who helped me greatly shortly after my job redundancy, announced that they were to fold and close later that December, due to insufficient funds. This story made the front page of the local, Gazette and Herald newspaper.

I felt it was my turn to help them. I set up a Twitter page, then called @SaveWiltsMind to get the attention of people who may not read the local papers and get the story of the imminent closure out to people and beyond the Wiltshire jurisdiction.

Within barely 2 weeks, the Twitter page gained enormous support with over 700 followers sending beautiful messages from across Britain, Ireland and beyond. Thankfully, the organisation was saved from closure via an anonymous donor who gave £50,000. Whether the donor came across the story via the Twitter page or not, I will never know. I ran the Twitter page for another 2-3 years on their behalf afterwards.

There is much, much more that I could have wrote about during the first 35 years of my life. Since 2012, my life has been chequered and marred by numerous setbacks that have included unpleasant neighbour disputes, my Mother battling Cancer and very sadly, the brutal murder of a friend.

I had to continually leave my flat during the latter part of 2016 and much of 2017 and stay at my parents house during most of this time and during my Mothers Cancer battle because of my then vulnerable neighbours flat was taken over: first by local yobs masquerading as friends and later on by more hardened and violent, 'County Lines' gangs; with loud music, fighting, drug dealing/using going on day and night. It was a truly horrendous time. The flat was completely vandalised once an eviction notice was granted and the damage took weeks to repair. I must have spent over £300 in total, during those very tough months, in taxi and bus fares, having to regularly leave my flat, often during the night.

Paul Treacy

I will be prepared to write more in detail about my life, especially after 2012, should I ever write another book. I even had brushes with the law myself though never got arrested.

As you will see from the quick life story I have given you, many, many people such as myself are forced to try much harder to get just half as far. There is so much fantastic potential and talent out there that is often locked and kept away. Hence, the Snakes and Ladders metaphor. Imagine if for example, the Jamaican athlete, Usain Bolt, was told just 2 minutes before a 400 metre sprint, that he had to don a rucksack with a sack of cement within it or else he will be disqualified from running.

Holding so many millions of people back and simply shrugging the issue as saying 'that's just the way it is', is gravely damaging for all of wider society as a whole.

PART THREE

The Culture of Denial

Since 1988, I have had numerous parts of my life completely ruined along the way and to be then told that I should actually take much of the blame for it: from secondary school and college to my places of work to the unpleasant neighbourhood situations that I had to suffer. The phone call I had from the agency back in 1996 as mentioned in the Toxic Mid-Nineties subchapter, seemed to represent just about everything at the heart of those who perpetrate, enable and excuse this abuse: The culture of denial. Complaints and grievances were usually met with "Yes, but…." At just about each and every turn.

You may have heard such spin talk conversations on TV, radio or even among people in general conversation. I will give you two such examples to explain things, much more further in this context of individuals who try to deny and make light of very serious allegations. Both of the following are based on factual events.

For example:

Several young military recruits took their own lives in recent months due to a rampant bullying culture at several, Army Barracks, across the country.

"Yes, but they obviously were not soldier material. You need to be toughened up in order to face being in the line of combat."

Some women who tried to forge careers as actresses and models have made allegations of sexual assaults and other forms of unwanted attention from aging, famous men in the Hollywood industry.

"Yes, but these women literally threw themselves against these guys in the pursuit of fame, so what do they expect??"

These are the typical kinds of responses that you will face from such people who always try to normalise the thuggish and unpleasant behaviour of others. Many perpetrators and enablers of abuse, literally view those with hidden and physical disabilities, as being some kind of subhuman species. Those who harbour such shocking levels of hatred and contempt can be found in every walk of life, the whole world over. These people are 'just doing their job' or there has been some kind of 'misunderstanding' along the way and always on the behalf of the complainant. This kind of gaslighting tactic is one that I have had to endure countless times through the years. No matter what you say or do, the blame will ultimately lie with you in the end.

You could have done this….You could have done that!

Why didn't YOU……at the time??

Yes, but YOU……

From the Wikipedia website: Gaslighting is a colloquialism, loosely defined as making someone question their own reality. The term may also be used to describe a person who presents a false narrative to another group or person which leads them to doubt their perceptions and become misled, disoriented or distressed.

And so it goes on.

Many people I know my age and older have had at least one job where they had an awful boss and/or supervisor and were hounded out or unfairly dismissed. And some of them are among the most friendly and trustworthy people that you could ever wish to meet.

Many Autistic and vulnerable people are often placed in a position where they are unable to defend themselves.

As long as you are turning up on time, doing the job you are paid for to a good standard and are of a polite and friendly nature then there should be absolutely no reason whatsoever for anyone to be giving you a hard time. I would strongly recommend to Autistic and vulnerable jobseekers to try and find employment with larger companies that have good reputations, especially in regards to promoting good wellbeing and mental health rather than anywhere that employs less than 35 people. (Unless you know of people working in such places that can vouch for the said firm being a good employer.) There are numerous, reliable webpages on this subject matter that are worth checking out.

So many small firms come and go within barely ten years and in so many cases, due to the senior staff and not because the regular staff who came and went during that time were unreliable as is often perceived. The body language of demoralised staff in toxic, working cultures speaks volumes as it did in the warehouse I had the huge misfortune of having to work at in 1994-95. The staff always looked totally fed up, their heads usually bowed in resignation before the start of the shift and the ashtrays on the tables would be full to the brim with cigarette butts by the end of it. Hardly surprising that most people who worked there, didn't stay there for that long.

There will always be those who will be in a total state of denial. You need only watch 'The Apprentice' (UK) TV programme for example, when an adequately qualified but socially incompetent candidate gets 'fired' by Lord Alan Sugar in the earliest stages. S/ he will always be in a rock solid, state of denial afterwards and question Lord Sugar's decision, even though he built up his multi Billion, Amstrad empire from scratch and question why he didn't fire another candidate, rather than on admitting their own failings. There are some people that you can never, ever reason with no matter how hard you try.

Sometimes in far more extreme cases, entire Corporations, Organisations and even Governments will be in denial over their grave failings and wrongdoings. It is a ghastly human trait and sin that has affected every part of History, one way or another. If you have an Autistic or vulnerable friend or relative or you know of anyone who is going through a very tough time in education, relationships or work, then please be there for them, listen and don't judge. Don't ever downplay anything unpleasant that they may be experiencing and dismiss it in any shape or form, even if everyone else is telling them to 'get a grip' and to just deal with it. Their mental health and wellbeing - And yours, are of Paramount importance. (In Britain, there are now tougher laws in place in regards to protecting workers from exploitation, discrimination and abuse, such as the Equality Act – 2010. Further details can be found online.)

Peter denies Jesus three times.

Shortly after Jesus was arrested after having been betrayed by Judas Iscariot, Peter denied three times that he was one of his disciples as Jesus foretold to him earlier that he would deny him. The following day, the Roman Governor, Pontius Pilate, when heckled and jeered at by a baying mob, demanded that Jesus be crucified, despite having committed no crimes and even after having had him beaten and scourged, Pilate then offered them the chance to release either Jesus or Barrabas, who was a notorious murderer, as it was a Jewish tradition for a prisoner to be pardoned during Passover. But the crowd before them demanded that Barrabas be released and still demanded the crucifixion of Jesus. After failing to change the mind of the crowd before him, Pilate, after having washed his hands before them, then instructed that Jesus was to be crucified. It is widely believed that Barabbas himself became a Christian in later life.

Hardened Attitues and Fairness in the Job Market

It seems that many Autistic children and adults have too often, been harshly and unfairly judged on their social and communication struggles, rather than focus on the many unique talents and skills that they already have to offer. Feelings of deep despair, low self-worth and self-esteem can run deep into an individual's psyche, on and off, lasting years or even decades, as it was in my own experience. Nobody in human history ever asked to be born - And no one gets any choice in whether or not they will have disabilities or illnesses of any kind, who their parents are and as to what their circumstances will be. No child should be given up on because of any kind of setbacks, hidden or visual, their background, who their parents are and the lifestyles that they themselves may lead.

All teaching staff in all types of schools the world over should, in my own opinion, be made to swear an oath, legally binding and signed on paper in that they will do their utmost for every child they teach, that they will be treated with respect and be given every chance to succeed. This is certainly not a form of political correctness, saying they should engage a softer approach. Teaching can be a tough task, which is fully understandable and I believe in maintaining discipline. However, installing a culture of being hard but fair, while being practical in working at solving problems when they arise rather than mocking and berating a child in full view of their classmates, because they have made mistakes, and/or are struggling with tasks at hand. No child, who is well behaved, should ever have to dread attending certain classes as I sometimes did. More forms of training aimed at helping Autistic and disadvantaged children and teenagers would go a long way too. No child should ever be held back. There are probably thousands of undiagnosed children out there. All teaching staff need to be made aware of the signs and not simply dismiss stimming and bizarre displays of emotion as bad and unruly behaviour. Any teacher who bullies or humiliates any child simply because they are struggling does their profession a huge disservice. A surgeon will give the same attention to detail to a man living in a trailer park as he would a millionaire. A mechanic too, will work just as hard on the clapped out Ford Mondeo as he would a nearly new, high performance Mercedes. Teaching children should be applied with the exact, same principle too, regardless of their backgrounds.

Far too many children and boys in particular who come from lower socio-economic backgrounds are often being failed terribly. Obviously, not everyone will leave school and go on to become music legends and sports stars but there is a huge array of talent, even among these kids that is never nurtured and just goes to waste. If, for some people, having to teach certain children/teenagers they despise because of their ethnicity and/or background - And having to sign an oath as part of training for and entering the teaching profession is a problem for them, then the teaching profession is simply not for them. There should be no compromise.

The English County of Wiltshire, where I am from and much of the surrounding area is mainly, rural, affluent and Conservative. There is an institutional stigma among many people in the County that those who struggle within better off parts of England such as this area, have only themselves to blame. To them, it is simply a combination of poor lifestyle choices and laziness.

This assumption could not be any further from the truth. There are a whole range of factors as to why people may fall on hard times. As well as job redundancies, situations such as illness, injuries, bereavement, mental health struggles and having to care for a relative are among the unforeseen circumstances that can affect absolutely anyone, anywhere.

While urban poverty such as that seen in London, Birmingham, Manchester and Glasgow is far more visible, rural poverty, which affects every county in Britain and Ireland, is much less so. The notion that a Central London millionaire works harder than a school janitor or supermarket cashier is absolutely ridiculous

With the current Pandemic in which many were furloughed and lost their jobs along with the closure of the Swindon based, Honda car plant in Summer 2021, resulting in hundreds of job losses, I hope and pray that attitudes towards people facing tough times will begin to change among many, in and around the Wiltshire area.

Depending on the situation and circumstances, some people are much more luckier than others in getting life back on track.

Likewise, people born with hidden and physical disabilities never asked to be the way they are and neither did they choose the often crushing circumstances that so many find themselves in through no fault of their own by being constantly marginalised to the fringes of society.

Now, I am NOT going to suggest that because around 1.15 - 1.5% of the adult population of Britain, Ireland, Australia and the United States have hidden disabilities, that around 1.15 - 1.5% of every single workforce, trade and profession have the same ratio among their ranks. This is just not practical and possible and I am fully aware of that. I am not in favour of the politically correct strategy (and oxymoron) known as 'positive discrimination' which is often adopted by certain corporations and I do firmly believe in hiring the right person for the job.

A fair percentage of people with hidden disabilities are not capable of working and another percentage can do so if specific adaptations are made - Which some companies cannot fulfil for a variety of reasons. Some jobs are totally unsuitable altogether.

Most people on the Autism Spectrum should be encouraged to give something a try and absolutely none should be bullied and coerced into doing something that they don't wish to do.

More adequate training and understanding is badly needed for careers advisers, schools, colleges and Job centre staff on these issues. There is so much to discuss on this topic which I would be more than happy to discuss with anyone up to Government level. Any company that has had a culture of bullying towards Autistic and vulnerable staff should face heavy fines via new laws and with prison sentences given to the worst offenders in extreme cases.

Even the most welcoming and understanding of employers may have to dismiss someone because they are overwhelmed and are struggling in their work. Job centre staff need to show more empathy and understanding and try to work towards more practical solutions in finding something more suitable if that is it all possible. No dismissal because of struggling in a previous job should ever blemish any future prospects.

Searching for jobs in the post Pandemic future will be very tough for so many people. In some cases, there will be unfairness at play with far less deserving people getting ahead by being hired and/or promoted. Us Brits often refer to this practice, which is often common in certain, elitist circles as being 'jobs for the boys.' (Eg: The spoiled brat, son of a CEO's golfing buddy with an over inflated ego and sense of entitlement, being hired for one of the top jobs.) Something that is not new, unfortunately.

Bad management, combined with staff not fit for their roles, brings poor decision making, toxic cultures, low morale, bullying and higher staff absenteeism. This in turn brings stress related illness, higher alcohol/drug use and higher divorce and family breakdown rates. The enormous tidal wide of human misery also costs Billions to the economies of dozens of nations across the globe every year. As mentioned earlier, many people, even some of the most friendliest people you could wish to meet, were hounded out of or unfairly dismissed from at least one job.

Even in the English Football (soccer) Leagues, which seems to be a microcosm of the modern jobs market, a team manager is now 3 times more likely to be sacked than they were in the 1960s. Many of those managers didn't deserve their dismissals and are often rash decisions by Club Directors.

Some managers go on to different clubs and in so many cases, go on to beat the side they were actually sacked from. Britain has often been referred to as 'The sick man of Europe' when in fact, in so many cases, it is the often, incompetent people at the top that so many good people are sick of.

The motor industry tycoon, Henry Ford, always insisted that treating all staff with respect, while providing decent wages and working conditions brought better productivity for any company, which of course was right. The Detroit built, 'Model T Ford' was the first car to be produced over one million times.

People with hidden disabilities, in many cases, are naturally more better in decision making than the general population, which goes a long way. Many such people under 35 should be actively encouraged to start their own business, provided that they have enough training, expertise and support from family and/or friends. (Maybe go into business along with a good friend?)

Plan everything well in advance beforehand and talk with more experienced people in your line of work whom you may know. The possibilities are endless in the modern, digital age, which was not around in my own childhood years. Do not let anyone tell you differently. If, like myself, you live in a less urban area of the country then you may wish to consider relocating to a larger town or city to further your career.

Post Pandemic UK will see some tough challenges ahead but please don't be discouraged. Here is a list of people diagnosed with or strongly believed to have been, on the Autism Spectrum: very amazing and gifted people. Some of whom have left a truly remarkable impact on World history.

Steve Jobs - Co founder of the Apple Computer company
Andy Warhol - Artist and cultural icon.
Albert Einstein - Scientist, Physicist, Mathematician.
Dan Aykroyd - American actor.
Darryl Hannah - American actress.
Sir Isaac Newton - Mathematician, astronomer and physicist.
Wolfgang Amadeus Mozart - Classical composer.
Lewis Carroll - Author of Alice in Wonderland.
Hans Christian Andersen - Children's author.
James Joyce - Author.
Nikola Tesla. - Inventor.

"If, by some magic, Autism had been eradicated from the face of the earth, then men would still be socialising in front of a wood fire at the entrance to a cave." – Dr Temple Grandin. Autistic Scientist and animal behaviourist.

Stepping Out of Your Comfort Zone

While I will be actively encouraging people with hidden disabilities to find out more about the Christian Faith and to give Church a try, I also want to try and encourage anyone reading this book to do the same, especially anyone who has been given a raw deal in life:

People who struggle with mental health issues.
Survivors of childhood, sexual abuse and/or domestic violence.
Former prison convicts. Especially those who are from troubled families and/or raised in the care system.
People recovering from addiction.

The list is not exhaustive. And it is not just about encouraging disadvantaged people to come to Church and for Churches to make reasonable adjustments. It is about going even further and encouraging Church Elders and even regular worshippers to offer continual support throughout. Vouching for people in careers, housing, further education and training.

And to NEVER give up on such people, even if you see them in the street intoxicated and/or have been made aware that they were recently arrested once again. Only in the most extreme situations and on Police advice where they may pose a risk to anyone at a Church, should you then keep away. Many of these people are lost souls and will have endured hard times and horrors that many of us simply cannot begin to image.

At this current time in 2021, many people will have been badly affected by the Pandemic, with many losing their jobs and concerned for their health and that of their family and friends, while also worrying what the future will bring.

The population of the whole planet has not faced a situation on such a grand scale since the Second World War of 1939-45.

Exactly how life will resume in the following years remains to be seen at this time but many more people in this secular age are now starting to ask the even bigger questions about life, even if they never discuss these questions among anyone in their closet circles.

Churches of all denominations need to be prepared of a possible new influx of people attending services and how best to welcome and accommodate them.

Throughout Part Three, I will be strongly encouraging all Christians to try and do their utmost in stepping out of their comfort zones. For some, like people who engage in charity work and helping homeless people for example, this will be an easier task and for others, it may come as a challenge.

When I have gone out for the day and spent an afternoon in one of the more urbanised areas closer to home (Bath, Bristol, Swindon) and have seen a caring, elderly man or woman take the time to talk and listen to a homeless or troubled man who is unkempt, heavily tattooed and has had a bit too much to drink - The very type of people who others will cross the road to avoid - I find it such a very heart-warming sight. Basic contact and small talk like this can make such a huge difference.

It will take time for some people to engage with anyone that they are not used to, which is perfectly understandable. We are only human after all.

Every Christian, regardless of colour, creed and status is under obligation to help less fortunate people in caring and practical ways that does not have to involve money. And to confront all forms of ignorant attitudes and injustice that hold such people back.

The evil regimes of enforced, racial segregation and rampant discrimination seen in the United States and South Africa throughout much of the 20th century was in part, dismantled by white allies, most of whom were driven by their Christian faith.

Many of these people will have endured beatings, damage to their property, shunned by their communities and in many cases, even their own Churches. (Many of these type of folk shared the distorted view held by those Governments, that segregation and restricted rights for Blacks was in the best interests of everyone.)

Those anti-racist, white Americans in the Deep South States of Georgia, Alabama and Mississippi in particular went FAR beyond stepping outside of their comfort zone. Many gave up their comfortable and respectable lives to challenge the status quo in the firm, Christian pursuit of campaigning for equal rights for all African Americans and other non-white minorities.

Although both countries still face huge challenges from within, it is reassuring that racist attitudes among white men and women born since 1997 is now far less prevalent.

Autistic and vulnerable folk can truly enrich any place of worship in the long term, provided they are given the best welcome and support possible, early on. When you look at things in the perspective of those White Christians who took a stand against Institutionalised bigotry, what I will be suggesting and encouraging is not really too much to ask. No regular, adult churchgoer has any excuse to not say as much as "Hello and welcome" to an Autistic/ vulnerable newcomer after 7 consecutive Sundays on the trot.

Autistic Youth Being Led Astray!

From this side of the Atlantic, I have been paying very close attention to many of the events that have been unfolding, most notably the events since the death of George Floyd in May 2020 by rogue, Minneapolis Police Officers, which was filmed by concerned onlookers and passers-by who repeatedly begged Officer Derek Chauvin to take his knee off Mr Floyd's neck. The aftermath brought on rioting, looting and burning throughout the city over the following days. Large scale, 'Black Lives Matter' marches took place throughout the United States and across the World, shortly after. Statues of Confederate War Generals and slave traders such as Robert E. Lee were pulled down. (The statue of slave merchant Edward Colston in Bristol, less than 25 miles from my hometown was also toppled and made International headlines. Every institution in the city bearing his name has since been renamed.)

Large scale disruptions in West Coast cities such as Portland and Berkeley, both of which are known to have a history with a strong core of militant, ultra-left students, boiled over once again. Later on, came the very much disputed, American Presidential elections with Joe Biden defeating Donald Trump in the quest for a second term as President. Disputes and fighting broke out in numerous polling stations in late 2020.

On January 6th 2021, countless thousands of Trump supporters turned up to Washington DC from across the country and shortly after Donald Trump gave an impassioned speech, thousands of disgruntled supporters made their way from the White House vicinity to the Capitol Building in truly shocking scenes that seen the crowd breaching security cordons and then managing to enter the building which sadly resulted in several deaths and many injuries. Over the years, many of us have seen such scenes unfold on news reports in Third World nations and even in European countries, where government buildings were breached or attempts were made to breach them, but I honestly don't think any of us ever imagined, even in our wildest dreams that such scenes could ever unfold at the House on the Hill: the home of Congress!

It is heart-breaking to see the nation that I have so much love and respect for, in spite of its flaws and problems, which I have long been familiar with from my earliest years, be blighted by even so much more division from within. (Many of my fellow Britons may not be aware that the whole, North American continent has been more at turmoil than they may realise.) Now, along with the seeming political tensions, there are other factors at play among the long standing, social issues such as inner-city poverty and racism that have long cursed various parts of this otherwise great nation - There is a rising opioid crisis both legal and illegal, devastating entire communities, many of which were once industrious and prosperous in more better days gone by. Much of the heroin and illicit drugs of all kinds that makes its way across the American border is brought across by ultra-violent, Mexican cartel gangs. Many of the unfortunate souls who try to illegally enter the United States from Mexico and other deeply troubled, Central American nations, in the search for a possible, better life, are more often than not, forced to smuggle drugs by the cartel gangs. The risks are truly enormous. Most of the major cities in the United States on the west coast in particular are now in some stages of terminal decline due to a number of factors with large scale homelessness and 'tent cities' on many blocks around

Los Angeles, Oakland and San Francisco. Whole areas suffering from terrible crime, alcohol/drug abuse, unsanitary conditions and widescale littering that would have been completely unimaginable during the middle of the 20th Century. And the problem continues to get even worse.

As if all of the events of 2020-21, combined with the pandemic were not bad enough, regular Christians across the United States and beyond were to discover, much to their horror, that one of America's most revered and respected televangelists, the Indian born Ravi Zacharias, who passed away in May 2020 after a Cancer battle, had been living a double life behind the scenes in his more later years, with many women from as far as Thailand, reporting that he had sexually assaulted them often during and after having been given, massages: And that he often justified himself in doing so, stating that he had greatly pleased God for his services over the years. Reporting him to the authorities he told them, would see many more souls descend into eternal damnation if he were to be arrested, tried and sent to prison – As he would be disgraced and would no longer be able to preach the gospel to larger numbers. (A mindset that is very common among wicked men in cults and remote, religious communities.)

Very understandably, these revelations have been absolutely devastating for Ravi's family, the staff at RZIM – Ravi Zacharias International Ministries and also for the many people who tuned in to his sermons and/or donated to RZIM over the years. The RZIM organisation has now ceased for good. I wish the staff all the very best of luck for the future.

The Boy Scouts of America at this time are undergoing a lawsuit by the many, many adult survivors of childhood abuse inflicted by scout masters who were trusted to look after them. The organisation may yet cease to exist due to the enormous compensation they may yet have to pay out to the survivors and the irreversible damage done to its reputation. (The British born movement has undoubtedly played a much larger role in general, American society than it has here in Britain: its nation of origin. This must obviously be heart-breaking news for the majority of good people who have ever been involved with the movement.) Across the border in Canada, the country and whole world are coming to terms with the horrors of mass graves being found of indigenous children near where state funded 'schools' that were run by the Catholic Church in order to assimilate such children into wider, westernised society and where violence and abuse, meted out by priests and nuns was rife. Several Catholic Churches across Canada have since been burned down in retaliation to the discovery of these graves.

On both sides of the Atlantic and further, there are yet more and more disturbing atrocities, revelations and scandals being discovered from ten, twenty, fifty and even one hundred years ago, on top of existing, current issues and challenges, all of which can be thoroughly upsetting and demoralising and that can truly shake our faith in human nature. And for some, faith in God. It is becoming ever more harder to know exactly as to who and what to trust these days.

The world that anyone who was born after 2000 will face, for so many, looks set to be a tough and uncertain one ahead. Those fortunate enough to live in strong and loving homes and one where the Christian Faith is central to their lives are among the far more luckier ones. Christians born within the first ten years of the 21st Century will need to play a very vital role in the way of helping lost and unfortunate souls, (which I will discuss further in the next subchapter) much more than the previous generations gone by – As for many, very unfortunately, there will be a fair percentage of vulnerable people and those on the Autism Spectrum, who will almost certainly have the odds stacked against them more than ever. In many places and the United States in particular, with the current social and political climate at highly charged, toxic levels not seen in the country since the American Civil War and with many more vulnerable and Autistic people will now be prone in getting lured into radicalised groups, gangs and unsavoury organisations more now than ever before.

I am not one to judge a book by its cover and would not tell anyone to steer clear of certain types of people, simply because of what they wear and/or because they may have numerous tattoos and/or piercings. Though I would strongly urge caution among the most extreme of examples. Growing up in 1980s England, I was never one to judge and neither were my liberal leaning parents. You would see very colourful types on a daily basis from punks to skinheads to fans of the New Romantic scene made popular by the likes of Boy George. (The huge majority, who were and maybe still into this 'way of life' as my Sister likes to describe it, including even those who may well have got on the wrong side of the law at some stage in their younger years, are decent, hardworking folk who have raised their own children reasonably well.)

However, there will be a small hardcore on both ends of the more radical, left/right scale who will try and lure impressionable and naive youth into their cause with many Autistic youth being possibly more at risk. Any decent human being, regardless of faith, colour and background, will want to see better equality, opportunity and fairness across the world. But, trying to achieve these aims with violence and trying to shut down any form of reasonable debate where others disagree such as in college campuses, in the practice known as 'no platforming' for example, is never the answer. While black lives obviously DO matter, as all lives do, the actual Black Lives Matter movement in itself has a militant and Marxist ethos. Sometimes, I check out tweets from individuals, such as the controversial Candace Owens, who is herself a black woman and who can see the fallacies from within the organisation and those similar to it. Then there is Antifa: the largest and most militant, left wing organisation which has no hierarchy or leadership as such but has members worldwide. I have watched numerous online videos, including those of freelance journalist and blogger Andy Ngo: an American man of Oriental origin, who has been on the receiving end of terrible verbal and physical abuse, despite causing no provocation of any kind when he has turned up to report on their demos and marches.

BLM and Antifa say they are united in fighting against fascism and racism – And it is true that all forms of discrimination need to be tackled head on – And also, that the historical horrors of the Transatlantic slave trade plus the slavery within America, Cuba, Jamaica and beyond in the subsequent years thereafter, must never be forgotten - And indeed, be taught within every education system at some stage. However, it seems as if the goalposts as to what actually constitutes as being fascism are being widened year on year.

Confronting burly and aggressive, white supremacists that wave Confederate flags and sieg-hiel in the streets to try and thump them is one thing but dishing out the same towards every-day, patriotic men and women who wear Stars and Stripes apparel (including MAGA – Make America Great Again - hats) and who are not out looking for trouble, is something else. To have voted for Donald Trump or to have voted for Brexit: British withdrawal from European Union membership, is even deemed as being 'fascist' to some! It must be duly noted that many people of all minorities voted for Donald Trump in the United States and for Brexit in Britain. Much of the left leaning media reported stories coming in from dozens of female, Polish and Lithuanian shop workers and waitresses, being falsely told by thoroughly unpleasant customers, that they will soon have to 'pack their bags and go back' in the weeks following the Brexit vote - However, these absolute morons do not represent the vast majority of the 17.4 million Brexit voters, many of whom themselves have friends and even spouses from different European and ethnic backgrounds.

To cry 'fascism' and 'racism' at just about everything and anything that some may happen to dislike and disagree with is a thoroughly deep insult to everyone who suffered and died over the years, because of genuine fascism and racism: from the black civil rights marchers who suffered regular beatings and police Brutality to the Six million Jews and other minorities who were killed during the Holocaust. The United States, whether people like it or not, is the backbone of 21st Century, western civilisation.

White supremacy beliefs of any kind, just as with like the ultra-left, are totally incompatible with the teachings of Jesus Christ. Whether in the run-down towns of the Appalachian region (USA) or in the remote regions of Eastern Europe, true Christ centred men and women need to strongly rebuke those with genuinely institutionalised, backward and abhorrent attitudes. There is only one race and that is the human race! God does not favour whites over blacks or vice versa. And God certainly does not favour anyone without any hidden and physical disabilities, either.

"Be not deceived: evil communications corrupt
good manners." 1 Corinthians 15:33

Every Church of every denomination, need to strongly agree to tackle such issues, whatever the social and political demographic of the region. The mere thought of hundreds and maybe possibly thousands of easily led, Autistic and vulnerable youth being 'cannon fodder' and ending up behind bars and having their lives ruined because of these lost causes and ruthless gangs preying on the weak for their own gains, is one that fills me with huge concern. Many of us will feel badly let down by our politicians on both sides of 'the pond' and beyond. Anger, bitterness and resentment can often boil over, as it did for me at one time. There are no magic wand and Hollywood speech solutions that can make absolutely everyone feel better. But to veer too far to the left or right, as history has already proven many times since the early 20th Century, becomes a very Slippery Slope indeed. We must keep an eye out for our youth and our Autistic and vulnerable youth especially, more than ever.

"It's easier to build strong children than to repair
broken men." – Frederick Douglas.

21st Century Born Christians – Power for Great Change

"Don't be discouraged at seemingly overwhelming odds in your desire to live and to help others live God's commandments. At times at may seem like David trying to fight Goliath. But remember, David did win." – David B. Haight.

Those among you, who were born any time during the first ten years of the 21st Century, who will be among the first wave of 21st Century born adults - And who also have a very firm and unshakeable faith in God: You guys have a truly huge role to play in helping those less fortunate than you are, especially anyone among your current age group. As mentioned in the previous subchapter, many Autistic and vulnerable youth are now more at risk than ever, by being exploited by callous individuals who certainly do not care for them and do not have their best interests at heart: the risks of being lured into and involved with extreme left/right wing gangs and movements that Jesus would certainly not approve of. Then there is the risk of being lured into drugs and gangs that distribute them and/or force vulnerable youngsters to become mules, as has become common with the 'County lines' scourge that has touched the majority of

British towns and cities since the mid 2010s. Vulnerable young women are at risk of exploitation by callous individuals with not so pleasant intentions.

The current social and political climate at this time of writing is extremely volatile in dozens of countries the world over. Communities and even families and friendships have been fractured by Politics, the emotionally charged subjects of the Coronavirus lockdowns/restrictions, vaccines, immigration, widening rich/poor divide, the education and healthcare system to name but a few. I truly feel badly for my 2004 born Son and his current generation, the entire world over, who have had to endure these lockdowns and restrictions and the enormous toll that this would have taken on their mental health and wellbeing, being robbed of what should have been some of the best days of their lives.

All of this, combined with the ever growing number of scandals, with many being of a sexual nature, involving Politicians, celebrities, police forces, banks, religious institutions and evangelical figures: It makes it so much harder to know exactly who you can really and truly trust in this day and age. For 21st Century born generations, it will undoubtedly be more easier for troubled youth to be lured into danger, crime and have their minds warped with poisonous ideologies. And it will be far more tougher in this current, modern age to convince such lost souls to renounce their ways and to turn to the Lord. It is a 'perfect storm', so to speak; and Satan will use these many widening divisions to his advantage in order to sow further discord, throughout the world. Many Christian raised youth will ultimately renounce their faith after they leave home. This is sadly something that is not new but looks set to become more highly likely over time. Even young men and women from the most loving Christian or even secular homes can end up being among the rising statistics for the year on year rising rates of mental health struggles, drug/alcohol abuse, victims of physical/sexual violence and suicides.

To you 21st Century born Christians and curious people - I cannot sugar coat this in any way: You are really going to have your work cut out and you will not be able to win everybody over to the truth. But don't 'beat yourself up' about it, so to speak. There will be plenty of times when you feel that you will not be able to make any kind of difference whatsoever but please try not to be discouraged. Always keep in regular touch with your Christian friends. And more so with your most devout friends, ministers and elders. Social media, text messaging and the internet is one huge advantage younger generations have which my own generation did not have in our more earlier years. Let them know how you are feeling and ask for prayer support and advice on any issues.

"Be of good courage and he shall strengthen your heart, all ye that hope in the Lord" Psalm 31:24

Keep an eye out for fellow students in school/college or at work, part or full time. If you see anyone who looks pale and withdrawn for whatever reason, try and take the time to talk to them. If you see anyone sat alone during breaktimes, either in the canteen, outside or anywhere else: someone who often seems to be on their own for much of the time, then please offer to talk to them and ask them how they are doing. If making these acts of Christian kindness are going to cause any kind of friction with your 'friends' then it is probably fair to say that they are not exactly genuine friends of yours anyway, judging by their disrespect. If you cannot reason with them and they sever ties with you then so be it. The same applies to any girlfriend or boyfriend that you may have and their own circle of friends. I strongly encourage you to date only Christians when it comes to relationships. It is while striving to become the best Christian you can be, (which is a more tougher feat) that you begin to see who your real friends are. By the time you reach your mid twenties, you will begin to see a lot less of most of the friends that you made during your childhood years if you haven't already left the area where you were raised by then. You will begin to gain a new and larger circle of friends along the way thereafter. That's just life.

Try to forge friendships with everyone at school, college and/or work whose circumstances have made their lives tougher than most. They may have very few or in some cases, nobody to turn to, during their day to day lives. Our youth and young adults need not end up leading crushing and chaotic lives like their own parent/s when there are fellow Christian students and colleagues that can offer them non-judgmental friendship and support. Don't forget to invite them to your Church and to remind them that they are always welcome. Encourage them whenever you see them, invite them to Evening Church services if there are any and mention that turning to Jesus is by far the greatest decision that they will ever make.

While you are at it, you too have to keep yourself sharp and focused: specifically in your spiritual and mental wellbeing. While there are the obvious vices to avoid such as heavy drinking, smoking, pornography, gambling and all kinds of illicit drugs from cannabis onwards, there are those more 'grey areas' that require even more closer attention, which can slowly drag you away from your Christian journey over a period of time.

Most Newspapers and forms of media:

The huge majority of Newspapers and news outlets, both on television and online are to be avoided at all costs, especially the downmarket, tabloid newspapers that almost always have a high content of sleaze and sexual imagery within them. Many spout regular and often hateful propaganda about vulnerable people being lazy and workshy, which as mentioned earlier, can lead to people being verbally and physically attacked in the streets or even on their own front doorstep. No genuine Christian should be buying such filth in the first place. And for any people to say they buy such papers to 'only' read the sports section or to collect coupons to get discounts for holidays and/or theme parks is just simply not excusable.

The same has to be said about beauty and celebrity magazines. A colossal waste of time and money. Much of the imagery within is often heavily filtered with the models often made to look more thinner than they actually are. So many teenage girls and young ladies struggle badly with self worth and self esteem issues in this modern age as it is. Around half, sometimes even more of the entire content within such magazines is just advertising. Again, usually with heavily filtered images. It is what you are like on the inside that truly matters.

Do not even so much as flick through these kinds of newspapers and magazines while in supermarkets or while waiting in a hair salon or barber shop. You will feel all the more better by completely shunning them from your life. Challenge your Christian friends if you happen to see them with any such content, in a polite but firm manner. Some may be of the notion that certain material like toxic propaganda and borderline soft porn 'is not so bad', which can lead to a slippery slope. The grey areas can so very easily lead someone into the path of regular sin, in much the same way cannabis usage often leads to more harder drug experimentation: and please remind them of this.

The same goes for all forms of so-called, Reality TV: total, mind numbing, over sexualised, toxic garbage - To be shunned at all costs. Be very careful not to get involved with any subculture that is dangerous: even those that are of no political persuasion. One such example is what is known in Britain as the 'boy racer' scene. There's nothing wrong with taking an interest in such cars and vehicles in general. In fact, mechanics and all forms of vehicle maintenance are truly great trades worth learning. But the temptation among young men and women to drive fast, while being involved in such groups, whether alone or competing among friends and rivals, and sometimes in urban areas, is always great. (The subculture has been highly glamorised by the multi Billion 'Fast and Furious' franchise since the turn of the Century.)

Very tragically, this can sometimes lead to tragedy. Four young men who lived 7 miles away from me, in the nearby town of Calne, all died in a horrendous, high speed crash in the area back in August 2020 which totally devastated their families and friends and with the tragedy making national headlines. If you can encourage any of your friends to renounce this subculture, you could potentially be saving lives. According to UK government statistics, 17-24 year olds are among the highest age category in fatal car crashes. With the exception of dense fields, woodlands, hills and valleys, there is barely a square mile in Britain where someone in that age bracket hasn't been killed on our roads at some time or another. The American Rock N' Roll singer, Eddie Cochran, had his fatal car crash in my hometown of Chippenham back in 1960 at the tender age of 21. There is a beautiful memorial on the local Bath Road at the very place where he had his crash. I see it on a near daily basis.

Any finally, back to the subjects of the hypocritical Woke Culture, Cancel Culture, calls to 'Defund the Police' and the others kinds of poisonous claptrap (such as telling children, there over 100 genders) that is currently 'making the rounds' in much of the education system around much of the western world: Don't ever be made to feel ashamed of who you are, your culture and faith. Phrases like 'White Privilege' only serve to cause more division, rather than unity. You need only to read the history books of how life was for so many millions of Britons and Europeans over many centuries to know how absolutely ludicrous the phrase, White Privilege, actually is. Over one million poor souls perished during the Irish, potato famine during the mid 19th Century – Some of whom were my ancestors. The grinding poverty in Victorian London, the then biggest city in the world, and this at the time when the Sun never set on the British Empire, is one that was the stuff of nightmares. No era throughout human history has ever been totally blissful and peaceful. Nor will it ever be so. Whatever you face, stand firm, and remember that the Lord will be with you, wherever you go. Always stay in the company of firm, like minded Christians.

'Blessed be God, even the Father of our Lord Jesus Christ, the Father of all mercies, and the God of all comfort: who comforteth us in all our tribulation, that we may be able to comfort them which are in any trouble, by the comfort wherewith we ourselves are comforted of God.'
2 Corinthians 1: 3-4.

Adaptations and Solutions

"And the King shall answer and say unto them, verily I say unto you, Insamuch as ye have done it unto one of the least of my brethren, ye shall have done it unto me." Matthew 25:40.

Different Churches, same goals.

All churches and places of worship are different. The suggestions I make may come across as patronising to some who will be totally adamant that their church is as friendly a place of worship as can possibly be. I will never be disputing any such claims.

There is no 'one size fits all' here. But whether you Christian folk worship at a 15th century, village church in Northumberland or at a 700 seated, converted cinema in South London, I truly hope and pray that all church elders with the greatest of respect, will try their best in understanding things from the Autistic perspective. If, a young Autistic man/woman has no car or any mode of transport and has struggled to settle in to every Church they have attended within a one mile radius of where they live, I simply cannot tell them to return and to 'try harder', next time round. For it is the regular worshippers, with all due respect, that need to try harder to accommodate them and help them on their potential, Christian journey.

Larger places of worship in more urban and cosmopolitan areas will obviously be at a far greater advantage to my suggestions. Any such church will almost certainly already have some Autistic adults and children plus people with physical disabilities and learning difficulties.

Trust.

Please realise, that encouraging anyone on the Autism Spectrum to attend a church service is one thing. Encouraging them to attend for a second, third time or more will be tougher in many cases. Many of these people will have been let down in so many ways, often by their families and by the system.

As tough and chequered as large parts of my own life have been, there are countless thousands, possibly millions of Autistic people out there who will have endured far worse, many of whom will have suffered, terrible bullying, physical and sexual abuse and will very often find it tough to build confidence and trust with new people.

Lanyards.

In recent years, some British supermarkets have introduced green lanyards with sunflower imagery upon them. Some have tags attached to them with laminated messages for staff and the wider public to know they have hidden disabilities and/or learning difficulties. If every regular, Autistic Christian would be willing and prepared to wear lanyards at services, it would put visitors with hidden disabilities at ease in knowing there are already people there who are similar to them.

Body language and reactions.

Even the most friendly of people may struggle in cropping up a conversation with an Autistic individual if they are not used to talking to them. Many people in wider society dismiss non eye contact, bowed heads and fidgeting as being disrespectful and rude, though this is not the case.

Neurological traits can often be very complicated and hard to understand. This will often require huge amounts of patience and empathy - And stepping outside of your comfort zone.

Your own reactions and body language will be vitally important. Crossed arms, eye rolling, sighing/tutting and hands on hips are extremely demoralising and discouraging. We have seen and heard these reactions, countless times over the years. Negativity of any kind could put off Autistic people from attending any future services altogether.

Well meaning Christians from other cultures often have a tendency to engage in physical contact, typically with arms across shoulders, hands on shoulders and hugs. This is vitally important: Please DO NOT do make any such contact with any Autistic newcomers! (Please ask if they would be comfortable for any such contact if they should continue to be attending services after around a few weeks.)

Discussions.

After introducing yourself, please strongly assure them that they are most welcome. Ask them some quick questions to begin with but nothing too deep and personal. Likewise, mention a bit about yourself. Some people with hidden disabilities open up about themselves more than others. If you happen to have any shared hobbies and interests then that will be very beneficial in developing friendships. If they mention for example that they support West Ham United in soccer (England) and/or New England Patriots in the NFL (USA) but you don't, then let them know of any Hammers or Patriots fans within the congregation if there are any and ask if they would like to be introduced to them sometime.

Church layouts and adjustments.

Every church is different in shape and size but reasonable adjustments can be made in each and every one. I would strongly suggest that a rear pew or row of seats on one side should be reserved for anyone with hidden disabilities and vulnerable visitors and regular worshippers, with individual seats placed around 7-8 inches apart from each other.

Please assure them that sitting in this particular section is merely optional but that there is no pressure to sit elsewhere, even if they regularly attend services. Any large church that has tables and chairs within (e.g.: in house cafe) should have one designated table for all vulnerable worshippers. Again, totally optional and with no pressure to join people on other tables.

Overwhelmed visitors.

Some Autistic visitors may feel overwhelmed during services with a whole range of different things: Being among so many new people, the singing, music, lighting, even crying babies and smaller children. Some may rush out to the toilet, sometimes more than once. Some may leave the church altogether.

Please bear in mind that church settings will be a whole new experience for many and that they may also become overwhelmed in numerous different settings like busy supermarkets and social events. Take note that they are NOT 'acting up' in any way.

Again, body language is vitally important. Displays of anger and disgust may discourage visitors from returning to your church and any other church in the future. Please reassure them that you fully understand, should anything like this ever occur. Some may need to visit the loo up to 4 times during a service, just through sheer nerves. Never, ever challenge anyone in any situation they may be struggling with.

Signage and training.

I truly hope, one day in the future, that there will be signage displayed outside places of worship, along with their websites and/or social media pages that they have ASC (Autism Spectrum Condition) friendly layouts and worshippers who have received basic, ASC awareness training in at least 25% of all places of worship who can help and guide them.

Elders and worshippers in smaller towns and rural locations should still make some forms of adjustments, regardless. Even if you don't know of any worshipper with Autism and one who is vulnerable. Any such person may still possibly visit your Church one day. The more welcome and at ease they feel, the more likely they are to return again.

Further resources and training are available via The National Autistic Society, (UK) Autistic Self Advocacy Network (USA) and other similar and renowned, national organisations.

Bottled water.

Every Church should have a multipack supply of bottled, mineral water on standby for every service. These can be bought very cheap from select supermarkets. Certain, larger churches do hand out mineral water to newcomers and visitors alike, along with 'Welcome, starter packs' containing basic information, which is always a great incentive. Some Autistic and vulnerable worshippers may find services during the Summer a real struggle. Always offer a chilled bottle in warmer weather. I often take 2 bottles to a Church service but can sometimes drink both before the service ends. Drinking more water increases concentration levels and helps to reduce levels of anxiety and stress.

Holding hands during prayer.

Whether in a line in the pews/rows or in a circle, the holding of hands, as in the case of hugs is one where many people with hidden disabilities may badly struggle with. Please respect their wishes if they do not wish to hold hands or are happy to do so, provided they are wearing gloves or have their hands tucked away into the sleeves of their sweaters or cardigans. Nobody should be pressured into having to hold hands with anyone.

Miscellaneous

There are certain other things that I feel need to be mentioned and that all Christians need to strongly take into consideration.

Many vulnerable worshippers are often not in a position to give any offerings every week when the collection is passed around. This can make some people feel very awkward and uncomfortable, regardless if the pastor assures people not to worry if they cannot donate.

When it comes to collections and offerings, I personally feel that it would be for the best if there was a collection box, either close to or within the foyer, as the congregation are leaving. Am sure the majority of worshippers would be comfortable with this idea.

There are some well meaning ministers who often have a tendency to continually ask the congregation to turn to the person sitting next to them and repeat a certain sentence s/he says. This can be very difficult and awkward for Autistic and vulnerable worshippers/visitors alike. I would kindly recommend that this pointless practice be phased out, especially if a church declares itself to be ASC friendly.

Every kind of out of church activity should also have adaptations for Autistic and vulnerable worshippers alike in order to help them feel fully included. Day trips and weekend retreats away may not be suitable, particularly for many 18-25 year olds. It varies from person to person.

House group studies may not be suitable for everyone either. Please bear this in mind, though suggest they are welcome to attend but can leave if they begin to feel overwhelmed.

Try and stay in touch with an Autistic or vulnerable person, even if they have been absent for a while or are reluctant to return again. Pray for them and strongly reassure them that they are always welcome to return if they feel comfortable enough and be willing to offer them your phone number/s.

Offer to meet them in the local park and/or for a coffee for a one to one chat if you can, especially if they are finding it hard to engage with others. As stated before, a small chat can make such a huge impact to someone's life. Always be willing to offer spiritual guidance and resources.

Whenever possible, offer to pick them up and drop them off home, should they live a fair distance from the church. Many will be reluctant to attend evening services and midweek activities during the darker months of the year for safety reasons.

If at all possible, try to liaise with family members and any social worker and/or mental health professional that they may be in regular contact with. It is not advisable to make any kind of home visit if they are from a volatile and dysfunctional family.

Families with Autistic children.

Always try to keep in mind what it is like for even the most loving families who raise children with hidden disabilities and those who may have children of adult age still living with them. Many will have faced exhausting times, often daily if their child is challenging, and will have endured scorn and resentment from neighbours, passers-by in the street and sometimes, even other family members, through the years, many of whom will have turned their backs on them. And also not to mention many emotionally charged meetings with social workers, teachers and local authorities. According to leading psychologists, many Mothers of Autistic children and children with special educational needs, often endure stress levels on a par of that, with soldiers in war zones. A full on child meltdown in a busy shopping mall is every young mothers worst nightmare, especially when other shoppers stop and begin to stare in disgust. The sights, sounds and even smells within a busy area like that of a shopping mall, can often be extremely challenging for young, Autistic children to be able to cope with.

Likewise, any young family with an Autistic child who may one day turn up who to Church and whose child may have a full on meltdown should not be met with angry looks and disdain. Meltdowns are not simply a case of the child deciding to be naughty or unruly. S/he may struggle coping and adapting to whole new environments and routines. In most cases, many Autistic children will eventually get used to a brand-new setting after 4-5 weeks and hopefully make new friends. All children of regular, Christian families, need to be encouraged to make the new, Autistic boy/girl feel as welcome as possible. Every Church should have a welcome and healthy core at its heart, thus making it feel like a true Family.

Autism and Relationships.

If you happen to have a teenage and/or young adult son or daughter and s/he were to tell you that s/he happens to be dating someone who is Autistic, it would probably put you a little bit on edge, which would be perfectly understandable. But you need not worry, as the overwhelming majority of such men and women are very pleasant, loyal, kind and caring individuals. Despite the struggles that they may have in certain, social situations and minor flaws/habits, Autistic people are far less likely to become verbally and physically abusive, far less likely to cheat, steal, bully and be controlling and manipulating towards their partners. Plus they are much less likely to pressure partners to have premarital sex and less likely to have any dependency towards alcohol and drugs. If s/he happens to be dating him/her long enough that you get to meet them, please understand that the first few meet ups may be a little awkward and strained to begin with. But please do not come to conclusions too soon. For most young men/women your son/ daughter is dating, this will gradually ease over time.

The more accepting and tolerant that parents, siblings, wider family members and close friends are the greater the chance that a strong and loving relationship can thrive. I have to be very honest here for any young Autistic people in early stages of relationships: Despite any of your best efforts, you will have to brace yourself that there is a strong possibility that the parents and siblings of whoever you are dating may not be accepting of you, even if you are reassured that they are 'very down to earth' people. In some instances, this may quickly fizzle away as they might just be a little bit 'old fashioned'. However, if they have less than tolerant attitudes that cannot be altered then please understand that it is them and not you that have a problem. If, whoever is dating you, breaks up with you because of family pressures, then shame on them. (And if any among them even profess to be Christians, then I personally, seriously have doubts to those claims.)

Autistic, young men and women often make for truly fantastic Husbands and Wives and also fantastic Mothers and Fathers, even if their own parents and families have failed them. While I will not claim to be an expert in relationships, I would strongly advise any young, Autistic men not to be too clingy and to not be romantic too often via constantly buying gifts due to any insecurities. Do not consider Marriage until you are at least 24 years old. It is best to concentrate on any studies/career progression and ambitions while focusing on planning your life ahead, before taking that giant leap. And also to firmly be in a position mentally, spiritually and financially to do so. It is best to be in a steady relationship for at least 3 years before even deciding to propose.

The notion of disability being a 'punishment' from God.

Throughout much of the Bible, particularly in much of the Old Testament, there are numerous instances of wicked nations and/or people being punished by God. The ten plagues of Egypt, during the time of Moses and Pharaoh is among one of the most well known examples. However, God never uses disability as a punishment towards anyone during birth because of the sins of their Parents, Grandparents or Forefathers from many years before. Anyone who may believe or theorise such things have been seriously misled or are misleading themselves. Such outdated views can cause huge distress for people with disabilities of all kinds, as well as their loved ones.

A percentage of Babies are unfortunately both with sicknesses, disabilities and deformities in many instances because of man made events, eg: chemical spillage or dumping in local water supply, Mothers injured during pregnancy or because of the unhealthy lifestyle of the Mother while pregnant.

In early 1999, the then England soccer manager, Glenn Hoddle, who had once played and managed Wiltshire's only professional side, Swindon Town, for a while during the early 1990s, gave an interview to The Times newspaper in which he was believed to have said that disability was a punishment from God: a form of 'karma' as it were, for the sins of a former life. However, in his latest book at this time, 'Playmaker', he insists that his opinions were misinterpreted by the interviewer. Nevertheless, he was still dismissed as England manager, very shortly after by the Football Association. Mr Hoddle still firmly denies that he held any such views. (He went on to manage several more domestic Clubs before becoming a TV match commentator.)

Distorted views and distorted Biblical views in particular, have been responsible for some truly shocking events in history. During the era of the African slave trade which began in the early Seventeenth Century, many merchants and plantation owners truly believed that black people had no souls, hence justifying their many cruel methods and actions during the transportation of slaves to the Americas/Caribbean and after, once those who survived the horrendous journey had arrived and were forced to work in the plantations. Many others also believed that dark skin was 'The mark of Cain' which was placed upon Cain, (the first ever murderer in history) by God after he killed his brother Abel, both of whom were the sons of Adam and Eve, and mentioned, though never explained as to what it was, in the first Biblical book of Genesis.

As to exactly WHY God allows disabilities both hidden and physical, to babies, even babies born to the most healthy, loving and devoted Christian Mothers and Families, is a subject matter that can be far more better explained by more seasoned theologians and older Christians who were born with disabilities. There are an array of highly rated Christian resources and books upon this subject matter.

But you don't LOOK Autistic!!

Here is a sentence that a good few Autistic people will have probably been told at some stage during their lives, myself included. I myself, don't really stand out on the outside, in comparison to my peers and general, regular, everyday people. There is no archetypal 'look' to anyone on the Autism Spectrum, as is often perceived by much of society. Such words can be very hurtful and unpleasant, even if said by anyone with the very best of intentions.

Autism and the Ministry.

There are a small core of people on the Spectrum who would and could make for truly fantastic Church ministers. Imagine if there were 300 extra such people throughout the United States and the most fervent Christian countries of Brazil, The Philippines and South Korea, along with 100 ASC ministers in dozens of nations across the world – And the impact that this could have. So many of these amazing young men and women are capable of gaining an encyclopaedic knowledge of Biblical scripture in a short space of time, Mark my words. Along with their typical enthusiasm, friendliness and genteel nature, they could possibly win the hearts and minds of tens of thousands of more people to the Lord.

All young men and women who wish to engage in mission work overseas, either as a gap year or for more longer periods of time should spend at least 12 months engaging with less fortunate people in their own communities beforehand. It could be in helping

Paul Treacy

with soup kitchen work for the homeless or befriending vulnerable/ disabled people in more deprived areas for several hours a week or month. Anyone who holds the outdated, deserving/undeserving poor mindset as mentioned earlier in 'England's Grim Underbelly' really needs to be educated on the facts regarding as to why people can end up in hard times. Anyone, who willingly refuses to accept these facts will certainly not be suitable for overseas mission work.

Additional Messages

Message to Autistic readers and their families.

No matter what you choose: Whether you decide to give Church a try or not - And whether you ultimately decide to turn your life to Jesus or not: I want you to know that I am fully on your side and in your corner. Many of you, who decide to attend church and stick at it will almost certainly make some fantastic friends for life.

Others may find it a struggle and you may need to attend several other churches before finding somewhere more suitable. Try and find a friend or relative who would be prepared to come along with you, especially if you may find it nerve wracking. Please try to attend at least 12 Sunday services. For many it will gradually get easier over time.

There is nothing wrong with being nervous. It only shows that you are human and it certainly does not make you weak. Never be too nervous to ask any questions that you may have.

Keep on going. Wishing you all the love and luck in the world. Never let your past, your setbacks and your circumstances stop you from what you want to be in life and what you wish to achieve. Never give up on your dreams. Always remember: You are made in God's image and he certainly does not love you and view you any less than anyone else. You mean much more to him than you could possibly imagine.

Paul Treacy

Messages to Church elders:

I hope that I have given you much food for thought on these matters and that the overwhelming majority of you will find my proposals and suggestions, reasonable enough. Am hoping that any such proposals will be put into practice sooner rather than later and that sometime in the near future, every large Church in Britain, Ireland and beyond will have at least one more Autistic worshipper.

Those Elders and regular worshippers among you with or who have, children or grandchildren with disabilities and chronic, medical conditions of all kinds will be fully aware of how tough and challenging life can be at times. By agreeing to these reasonable adjustments and proposals, even if you don't think they will be needed, you will be doing your Church and the wider community as a whole, an even greater service.

Always be very careful in what you say, how you act and react towards Autistic people. It can only literally take just a matter of seconds for someone to be completely discouraged and demoralised – And put off church services for months, years or possibly for life. As in the parable of the Lost Sheep as mentioned in Matthew 18: 12-14:

How think ye? if a man have an hundred sheep, and one of them be gone astray, doth he not leave the ninety and nine, and goeth into the mountains, and seeketh that which is gone astray?

And if so be that he find it, verily I say unto you, he rejoiceth more of that sheep, than of the ninety and nine which went not astray.

Even so it is not the will of your Father which is in heaven, that one of these little ones should perish.

Search for anyone who has been long term absent from your local Church. And try your best in encouraging to return.

Sorry seems to be the hardest word.

If you have ever willingly given any Autistic people a hard and unpleasant time: whether or not you knew they were Autistic and whether or not they knew that they were Autistic at the time, then please do the right thing by getting in touch with these individuals and apologise for your words and actions. Even if you are in retirement age and you may have picked on someone during your school days. Even if you are a small business owner who should have hired the Autistic guy, desperate to find work over the less reliable individual you chose instead and then dismissed barely a year afterwards. If you see them in the street then please do the decent thing and apologise up front. If you are able to contact them by phone or via social media then do it that way. I am not going to hold my breath and be expecting scores of people to apologise to me. However, I wish to take this opportunity to apologise to anyone who I may have upset during moments when I was not so pleasant myself, from my childhood through to my adult years for whatever reason it was. There were many occasions when it was tough not to 'lose it' at times because of continually being held back and misunderstood. These days, as I am getting older and hopefully more wiser, I now exercise far better self control and walk away from any heated situations that may arise.

It's been emotional!

These three words are among the most well known lines ever spoken by a film character in British film history: and the final words spoken by 'Big Chris' in the 1990s cult gang flick, Lock, Stock and Two Smoking Barrels: played by the hot headed, former (original) Wimbledon FC and Chelsea soccer star, Vinnie Jones. And I felt that these three words were most appropriate to describe how life has turned out for me, thus far.

I have been fortunate to have attended numerous, 'high end' events where Mayors and local, influential people have been present. I even got to meet Prince Edward while volunteering for the Doorway Project in 2009. Over the years I have had some very unique experiences: I visited the World Trade Center during my New York visit, have seen Brazilian Internationals score goals for Real Madrid at their magnificent, Santiago Bernabeu Stadium, have visited the Roman Colosseum, stood at where Pope John Paul II, spoke to and gave Mass, in the presence of over a million people in Phoenix Park, Dublin Ireland, during his 1979 visit and have enjoyed being very close up to the Niagara Falls.

And yet, despite my skills and talents, despite the fact, I have visited many places and have experienced different cultures, I still continue to face a completely undeserved, uphill battle, against both a broken system and broken society, which will no doubt probably continue in one form or another until my very last breath on this earth, often feeling exhausted, angry and frustrated by the toll that continuous exclusion and being forced to endure a half-baked life for most of the year round can bring about on the mental health and general wellbeing for Autistic people. Life is rigged against us in so many ways, right from the start. And it should never be this way. At this time, I have still yet to Marry and own a House. Something I am still eager to achieve. How the life of someone on the Autism Spectrum turns out, will also vary according to social demographics, their background and the support (or lack of) by parents, teachers and employers.

In many instances from my primary school years until my mid-thirties, I have been mocked, humiliated and even threatened with violence. (Going to a 'Work Programme' meeting in 2013, I was patronised by the awful woman in charge, in front of over a dozen people by being sarcastically told well done in that I play a 'small part' in the HEALS organisation.) During my Facebook years, I couldn't help but notice that there were several dozen people that had 20 or more 'friends in common' with me in the 'people you may know' category that was a very regular feature on my profile screens. A few people, who didn't take too kindly to me in earlier times did eventually become friends with me. Hope and pray that if any of these willingly, less tolerant people should ever have children or grandchildren diagnosed with Autism and/or other conditions or vulnerabilities, that they will not view them any less.

While I will never claim to be the 'Nelson Mandela' for Autistic/vulnerable people, I will continue to fight hard for anyone who has the odds stacked against them and help in any which way I possibly can.

We just want to be respected and valued.

Hand on heart, I am not asking that Autistic people be given any major kind of special treatment. I do not wish to see huge amounts of Autistic symbols, flags and imagery adorned on Government websites, buildings, Police Cars and School/College campuses from Los Angeles to London to Sydney. I do not want to see 'sticking plaster' gestures like online hashtags and feelgood gestures from sports stars and celebrities, every now and then, however well-intentioned that they may be. We wish to see practical solutions towards our needs to make our lives and the lives of our loved ones, more bearable and easier in absolutely every shape and form that is practically possible and viable. More apprenticeships and scholarships, specifically designed towards Autistic teenagers and young Adults, would go a long way. And for us to be respected and valued more in wider society. There are more Autistic people currently on this planet than at any other time in world history. And there will be even more yet to come in the future. Indeed, by the end of the 2020s, huge swathes of the United States in particular will more than likely see areas where Counties and possibly even whole US States, where as much as 5% of the population will be Autistic. From the most powerful people in the world to the everyday man and woman on the street, everyone needs to help make a difference. So many everyday people need educating on these matters. And Christ centred people throughout the world can be at the very forefront of making great changes for the better.

Conclusion

These things I have spoken unto you, that in me ye might have peace. In the world ye shall have tribulation: but be of good cheer; I have overcome the world." John 16:33

Mainland Great Britain is very highly unlikely to ever become the fervent, Christian powerhouse it once was, prior to the World Wars. At the height of the Victorian era, churches would be packed to the rafters and missionaries such as Sir David Livingstone, often spent long periods of time in unchartered territory, deep in the wilderness of Africa to bring about the news of the Gospel to the many tribes there. The reason that the Christian Faith is so strong in much of sub Saharan Africa can be attributed to such brave men, who also played a huge role in the abolition of slavery, which was still very widespread within the continent at the time.

At this current time of writing, the statistics and figures for the ten yearly, 2021 UK Census, have not yet been made public. However, it is more than likely that many more people will have ticked the 'no religion' box, while some people of a more eccentric nature will identify themselves as being 'Jedi' or similar in the 'other, please specify' category. Dozens of some of Britain's most well-known figures in entertainment, literature and music to name but a few genres, have confessed to being atheists, some of whom have often spoke at length about their atheism to newspapers, University Unions and secular humanist organisation, conferences. (Common topics often include Catholic Church, sex abuse covers ups and gay/ lesbian persecution in Third World nations, both of which are truly horrendous and inexcusable.) Combined with the growing number of disbelievers, the faiths of Islam, Hinduism and Buddhism are also growing in number upon these shores, especially as the country has become more diverse over the last half century.

The older folk in my neighbourhood, during my childhood years, may not have ever talked about God to me and/or my friends but not one of them ever insisted that they disbelieved in the God of the Bible, either. And this despite what Britain and Europe suffered during their earlier years in the War. I personally think that most of them privately had some kind of faith. And I believe that the same could be said of my parents generation, commonly known as the 'baby boomers' who were very often born into large families following the mid 1940s.

As for my generation, known as 'Generation X' and 'Generation Z', the next generation, there are some positive signs that the Christian faith from Lands End to John O Groats, is not on its 'last legs' as some might think: Larger and regular Churches in Britain's 25 or so largest cities and also larger towns are still very well attended and more often than not, by young families, and some hailing from dozens of nationalities the world over. Many, well renowned organisations and charities such as Christians Against Poverty continue to make such a positive impact in helping the lives of many people facing hardship and debt in some of the most deprived areas of the country. Done with love and without judgement.

In this current age of great uncertainty, many young men and women will often quote that someone who was close to them who has since passed away is 'watching over them' during tough and challenging times and when trying to achieve or having achieved, personal accomplishments. "My Nan is watching over me...." has been quoted so many times by contestants, usually young women under 25, in televised, music and talent shows, over the years. The thought of an afterlife with peace and being reunited with departed loved ones, brings hope and reassurance to millions of agnostic and undecided people, even in far more secularised countries such as China and France.

There are a growing number of men and women who are having tattoos done that are of a Biblical theme: Imagery of praying hands, doves, crowns, scriptures and even of Christ himself. One former neighbour of mine had the exact tattoo of Jesus that David Beckham had done. (At this current time, David Beckham's son, Romeo, just so happens to be dating a young lady from my hometown.) Many Premiership soccer players and sports stars since have at least one Biblically themed tattoo. Such designs were very rarely seen in my Father's generation, even among heavily tattooed men. Friends of my Dad who were inked, typically had images usually consisting of wild animals, sparrows and names like 'Mum' and 'Elvis'.

Many more young men and women are gradually beginning to shun or reduce alcohol usage and shun drug use completely in favour of more healthier lifestyles, which is a positive sign too. There are many more people out there in the current generation who would be open to discussing the Christian Faith if the subject were to arise. Many more older men and women, whose lives have been blighted by alcohol and/or drug abuse are starting to ask those bigger questions too, especially with their family lives having been damaged and watching many friends die from their addictions over the years. Any 'highs' they may have enjoyed from their excesses in earlier times, simply cannot be reached again, no matter how hard they try. (The drummer, Mick Fleetwood of Fleetwood Mac fame is widely believed to have consumed enough Cocaine to have stretched a grand total of 7 miles, over the years! It is such a shame that this very likeable Englishman and so many others like him in the world of entertainment and music, went down such long and destructive routes.)

Millions of Britons have a Bible in their home, even if it has been gathering dust on the shelf for years and most people will have at least one Christian friend, work colleague or classmate. And although marriage rates have declined over the years, traditional Church weddings are still very popular among young couples who do tie the knot, regardless of their beliefs. Some may think that being a Christian is for 'softies' but there are some seriously tough fellas out there who hold a strong faith: Bear Grylls the adventurer, Tyson Fury the gypsy boxer, Paddy Doherty, likewise, is also from a very tough, gypsy background and Pastor Mick Fleming from Burnley Lancashire - The former gangster turned Vicar who regularly goes above and beyond to give a helping hand to some of the most hard up people within his local community. Although it was very sad to see Michael Sleggs of BBC comedy 'This Country' mockumentary fame (based 30-35 miles from my hometown, in and around the village of Northleach in nearby Gloucestershire) pass away from Cancer aged 33 in July 2019, it was truly reassuring to know that he eventually returned to his Christian Faith.

Whether people like it or not, Great Britain: it's history, culture, legislation, science, arts and impact on the rest of the world, were mainly shaped and influenced over the centuries by Christian values. Every nation where English is the first language and many Commonwealth nations have been hugely influenced by this land. And, this nation would be far worse without those values. For this reason, mainstream British society, though far from perfect, is overall, much more welcoming and tolerant than a great deal of the world and even in much of Continental Europe, where life for the less fortunate can be truly terrible for some. Trying to replace these values with something else, such as this divisive 'Woke' nonsense or another ideology, will never, ever be a substitute.

There are no quick fix solutions but I hope and pray that my son Joseph and the majority of Autistic people in his generation and the generations to come will not have to endure as much as 25% of what I have been through over the years. However, I am fully aware that many will still face unfair challenges and situations throughout their lives.

The System here in the UK is still very deeply flawed in certain areas and does not work in the best interests of many people. The Government and political parties of all persuasions, still have a long way to go. Much urgent reform and understanding is needed on these often, complicated issues.

Education and emphasis on the subject of hidden disabilities and mental health issues - And how so many people can often be held back through life, needs to be taught to children at least once a year from the age of 8 years old, onwards. More people representing ASC and Mental health organisations, visiting schools, colleges and even universities on a more regular basis would help to challenge institutional stigmas and stereotypes.

You can judge a nation by how it treats its most hard up and vulnerable citizens. Huge progress has been made by organisations and individuals alike since the turn of the 21st century but again, there is still some way to go. Attitudes are changing for the better in some quarters. Some may have read about my earlier life experiences and simply say 'well, that was then' and that I need not worry anymore. Living in less urbanised areas more often than not, typically harbours more discriminatory attitudes among its citizens.

People of all disabilities and ethnic minorities may not face the discrimination that their parents and earlier generations faced but sadly, certain toxic attitudes have faded, only to be overtaken by other, toxic attitudes. Since the turn of the century, with the rise of the Internet and social media, there has been a new rising tide of selfishness and hedonism: Rampant, sexualisation, consumerism and materialism. Trying to look your best, have the nicest of things and gain as many 'likes' as possible, is driving a new mental health crisis among our young folk and sadly, many are at risk of exploitation, abuse and being lured into gangs. Dangerous and destructive kinds of lifestyles are encouraged, plaguing the minds of so many people via social media and often by terrible role models.

There was one very sad story which to me, represented everything wrong with modern British and Western society in this era: the tragic case of the famous socialite, Tara Palmer-Tomkinson. This beautiful but often troubled lady had rubbed shoulders with countless rich and famous people throughout her life and was the goddaughter of Prince Charles.

She died in her London penthouse in February 2017, aged 45 from a perforated stomach ulcer and had remained undiscovered for around 5 days until her cleaner turned up for work. Just how someone, who became a household name, who was the life and soul of the party at the most exclusive clubs and holiday resorts in the world, never even had ONE soul who wondered why she had been so quiet during that 5 day time frame and who never thumped at her door after so many of their calls and texts went unanswered - Did anyone even bother to contact her during that time frame??

This tragic case was such a very sad sign of our times. It is terrible enough when an old lady twice her age suffers a similar fate, let alone someone who supposedly had the world at her feet. No matter who you are, ditch anyone from your inner circle who you know deep down, will never enrich your life. Be with people that will bring out the best in you, who will always have your best interests at heart and who genuinely care and support you through thick and thin. And have at least 3-4 VERY good friends throughout your life who WILL make that call and who will turn up to your door if they haven't heard from you, especially if you live miles away from any close family.

I have gained much hope and inspiration from our diligent, National Health Service staff during these current, challenging times and from both Prince Philip and Sir Tom Moore, who gave this nation a combined total of just over 200 years of outstanding service. I hope and pray that a greater and compassionate nation will arise such as that seen in the era which rose from the ashes, straight after Hitler's Germany was defeated in 1945. Three years later in 1948, despite the horrors and mass devastation caused, during the War, the Nation Health Service was founded and London was the first City to host the post-war, Olympic Games.

"For I reckon that the sufferings of this present
time are not worthy to be compared with the glory
which shall be revealed in us." Romans 8: 18.

We need to ask more than ever, what kind of a world do we want
our future generations to grow up in? Do we want a world where
narcissists and borderline sociopaths rule the roost and who insist
that current structures are as good as they can get and are here to
stay. That trying to be the best is the cornerstone of life, above all
else and that marginalised people are merely burdensome and aren't
worth worrying about.

Or we can have a world where fairness, acceptance, meritocracy
and kindness prevails. A better world and one spearheaded by men
and women with the love of Jesus, firmly in their hearts.

Extra: Becoming A Christian

When the 41 year old Basketball legend, Kobe Bryant, woke up, got out of bed and made his breakfast on the morning of Sunday 26th January 2020, little did he know that he would be doing this for the very last time. In total contrast to Tara, whom I mentioned about in the conclusion, he was among people he loved, was in full health and in good spirits as he and a group of others boarded a helicopter to attend a Basketball tournament in the Californian City of Thousand Oaks that his daughter Gianna, also a passenger, would be participating in that day. Tragically, the helicopter crashed in the hills near the town of Calabasas, killing everyone on board.

At current levels, around 150,000 people die across the world every single DAY. That is more than the population of Ipswich in England.

Among that number, a large percentage are of people who very sadly will never reach their 50th Birthday. Tomorrow is never guaranteed for anyone, no matter who you are or where you are from. We will all have to face death eventually, after which there are just two places to go from there: Heaven and Hell - And both last for eternity.

Hell, as described by Jesus in Matthew 13:42: "And shall cast them into a furnace of fire: there shall be weeping and gnashing of teeth."

This is a place you would never want to spend even just a few seconds in, let alone eternity! Those who enter will never escape. Spending a whole year in one of the most toughest and unpleasant prisons on this face of this planet would be far more easier than spending a single day in Hell, I can strongly assure you.

Jesus Christ is THE way to Heaven!

"For God so loved the world that he gave his only begotten son, that whosoever believeth in him should not perish but have eternal life." John 3:16.

From the moment Adam and Eve brought sin into the world in the first Biblical book of Genesis by disobeying God, following generations have since has waged and encountered violence, war, greed, abuse and suffering of every horrendous kind, which carries on to this present day. This was never part of God's intended plan for mankind.

Man cannot enter Heaven by good deeds alone. Believing that you are 'nice enough' will not suffice entry into Heaven. Only by the suffering of Jesus on the cross where he took our sins and paid the price for our iniquities can we truly re-establish unity with God and eternal life with the Lord of the Universe.

"Jesus saith unto him, I am the way, the truth and the life: no man cometh unto the Father but through me." John 14:6.

To become a Christian, please pray the following:

"Dear Heavenly Father, I realise that I am a sinner and that I have fallen way short of your standards. I realise that Jesus is the true son of God and that he suffered on the cross for me. Please forgive me and enter into my life. Renew my heart and take centre of my life. In Jesus' mighty name, Amen."

If you have prayed this prayer and have really meant it, deep in your heart, then Congratulations! You are now a Christian. This does not guarantee that the rest of your earthly life will be a bed of roses but you can feel reassured that you have secured eternal life with Jesus in Heaven. Please take the time to say another prayer in which to thank him, shortly after.

Christianity is not 'religion' but a relationship with God. Please tell others about your new faith and commitment. Read the Bible daily and find a good, local Church in your area. You may wish to visit several before you settle down.

God bless. Wishing you all the very best.

Printed in the United States
by Baker & Taylor Publisher Services